FULFILLING THE PROMISE

FULFILLING THE PROMISE

Reimagining School Counseling to
Advance Student Success

MANDY SAVITZ-ROMER

HARVARD EDUCATION PRESS

CAMBRIDGE, MASSACHUSETTS

Paperback ISBN 978-1-68253-353-6
Library Edition ISBN 978-1-68253-354-3

Library of Congress Cataloging-in-Publication data is on file.

Published by Harvard Education Press,
an imprint of the Harvard Education Publishing Group

Harvard Education Press
8 Story Street
Cambridge, MA 02138

Cover Design: Endpaper Studio
Cover Image: MirageC/Moment/Getty Images

The typefaces used in this book are Minion Pro for text and Univers for display.

CONTENTS

INTRODUCTION

A Profession Ready for Change

As a school counselor and university professor who trains future counselors, I hear one question over and over again from colleagues: "What do school counselors actually do?" People are often surprised to learn that school counselors support a wide range of student and school achievements and that they hold master's degrees. They are surprised to hear that in some districts one counselor has to support more than eight hundred students. They also are particularly surprised to hear that counselors are a promising but untapped resource to meet the growing demands on schools and the increasing needs of students in our society.

Over the past several decades, policy makers and the public have called on schools to fulfill their core goal of developing students' academic skills and address a wide range of societal priorities and student needs. This demand has been shaped by the growing recognition that students' social, emotional, and academic needs are intertwined and must be addressed as such. Expectations for schools have evolved to include screening for mental health problems, addressing barriers to learning, and ensuring that all students graduate college- and career-ready. These demands have been driven in part by the logic of streamlining support systems so students don't fall through the cracks of disconnected services. Meeting this myriad of expectations has left many schools struggling and overwhelmed.

Academic development is, of course, the core mission of schools. Even in this domain, however, schools are facing new challenges. Fueled by an education reform movement that has been laser-focused on identifying achievement gaps for groups of students, schools have been concentrating on identifying and supporting students who have historically not been served well by schools. Educators are working tirelessly to identify appropriate academic interventions, skill-building opportunities, and strategies that help students create links between classwork and future goals. Meeting these academic expectations is a significant challenge.

While academic expectations have grown, schools have also been asked to embrace the responsibility for supporting the social and emotional development of students. Currently, schools often say they are educating the "whole child" but are not yet proficient in developing the social and emotional skills that underlie academic achievement, creating positive school climates that foster engagement and belonging, or conducting screenings for mental health concerns that can get in the way of learning or contribute to unsafe learning environments. In fact, although many school leaders recognize that some students are struggling with anxiety and depression, they are challenged to consistently provide supports for managing these debilitating conditions.

In addition to calls for increased academic standards and attention to the whole child, schools have been under pressure to prepare students for success in college, career, and life. Across elementary, middle, and high schools, principals have been searching for new ways to engage students in career and college exploration and readiness activities. Schools have been asked to adopt college-going cultures, expand career and technical education, align high school and college curricula, support postsecondary planning, and ensure that all students graduate with a postsecondary plan. While at one time high schools were focused on graduation rates, today they are being held accountable for post-high school outcomes and, as a result, are looking for ways to do more, often with fewer resources.

Many school leaders feel daunted by the formidable task of meeting students' diverse needs across these three domains—academic, social emotional, and postsecondary. However, too often they overlook the fact that our nation's schools already have an untapped resource for address-ing these needs: school counselors. School counselors are trained to provide support to students across academic, college and career, and per-sonal domains. In fact, the school counseling profession has evolved over the past six decades to the point where counselors have become uniquely situated at the nexus of students' educational experiences. Yet, they are among the most underutilized personnel in education, due to a range of factors from extremely high caseloads to a system that has not realized their full potential.

In my work, I have learned that too many adults have negative per-ceptions of school counselors. I have heard accomplished people give speeches that begin with a story about a high school guidance counselor who told them they "would never amount to anything." These stories make for great drama and the situations were undoubtedly painful for the people who lived them, but they are the exception rather than the rule. The majority of school counselors I have met are highly skilled, are long-ing for change, and have been working hard to meet the high expecta-tions they have set for themselves. Many of us had a negative experience with a teacher or administrator along our educational journeys, but we don't tend to write off the value of all teachers or principals. Of course, as in any profession, some school counselors have languished in their roles as a result of inadequate training, low expectations, and a lack of support. Unfortunately, negative depictions of counselors have bled into popular media, creating low expectations of counselors that deter students, fami-lies, and educational partners and leaders from leveraging all that school counselors have to offer.

All these stakeholders should know that counselors are eager to be called on to help, and energizing evidence of their impact exists across all three domains. In the academic domain, studies highlight the impact school counselors have on organizational and social skills, attendance, and even improved standardized test scores.[1] Strong school counsel-ing programs have successfully contributed to reduced discipline rates, improved attitudes about school, a sense of belonging, and reduced referrals to special education.[2] Studies also show that counselor involvement leads to improved postsecondary outcomes. For example, research has shown that adding a single counselor to a school can increase college-going rates by ten percentage points and that students who meet with their school counselor to plan for college are more likely to take the important steps necessary to enroll and succeed in college.[3] According to this growing body of scholarship, school counselors have managed to have quite an impact in spite of low expectations and a host of organizational challenges. Just imagine what they could do with a more clearly defined role and the institutional supports to fulfill it!

School counselors' effectiveness is due, in part, to the hard work that has gone on within the field of school counseling. With leadership from professional associations such as the American School Counselor Association (ASCA), the College Board, and school counseling scholars and leaders, school counseling practices have benefitted from a set of national standards, evidence-based school counseling tools, enhanced cultural competence, best practice programming, and alignment with related professional competencies. However, these professional advances are largely invisible to educators outside the profession. School and district leaders as well as community partners have not been engaged in school counseling reform and have not educated themselves about successful school counseling initiatives such as data-driven school counseling, counselor-principal agreements, and postsecondary leadership teams. As a result, efforts to capitalize on the potential contributions of counselors are thwarted by uninformed leadership and conditions that are not conducive to counselor effectiveness. High caseloads, ambiguous roles, lack of organizational alignment between counselors and school mission, inadequate professional support from districts, misuse of time, and an overreliance on enrichment and add-on programming have strained a profession suited to support schools. Despite this reality, school counselors *could* become more effective if we conceptualize this problem as an organizational issue rather than a personnel problem. Educational leaders need to create the structural conditions for counselors to perform their jobs optimally. Reducing high caseloads is a good first step and has been often recommended, but it is not enough. Placing more counselors in an outdated role will not go very far to improve schools' ability to meet students' comprehensive needs. Our students need us to do more. They need us to unlock the potential of professionals who are right around the corner and ready to help.

A REENVISIONING OF SCHOOL COUNSELING—NOT JUST FOR COUNSELORS

This book provides an inside look at what is possible when schools and districts draw on the talents of their counselors and put them at the center of students' school experience. It provides a strategic and systemic approach to school counseling that enables educational leaders to draw on staff they already have to create supportive contexts and programs for students. In this approach, counselors are at the hub of student supports—their "academic home"—connecting and coordinating services much like primary care physicians coordinate patient care in medical settings. In a "medical home" model, primary care physicians are the first point of contact, provide as much care as is possible and reasonable, and refer patients for specialized care when needed. This book outlines the metaphor of the "academic home," in which school counselors are a first point of contact for student support and weave a web of networked supports so that students don't fall between the cracks. Although teachers may see themselves as students' academic home, the relationship students and teachers have with counselors is central to students' overall educational experience and success. By drawing on promising practices in schools, districts, states, and by individual school counselors and leaders, this book offers a conceptualization of school counseling that is not just for counselors but also for the district and school leaders, teachers, community partners, policy makers, and funders who shape the contexts in which we all work and students learn.

This book is written for anyone who believes that we can do a better job of supporting students and is willing to look carefully at the system. It is for educators who know that meeting the needs of all students requires tackling the hardest part—the structures and systems in which counselors work and are trained. Schools are systems, even if not visible to the naked eye. Everyone involved is needed to change the system and achieve better results. We know that schools need improved support services to promote students' academic, social emotional, and postsecondary development. We've tried adding new programs to "augment," "complement," "supplement," or even "compensate" for school counseling weaknesses. This book presents, instead, a perspective for strengthening school counseling. With a stronger system and the support of those extra community partners and programs, we can provide academic homes that equip all students with skills for success.

The book is also intended for content teachers, college advisors, and others wondering how improvements to school counseling can provide support for achieving their own goals. These professionals, who work in and outside school buildings, often hand in hand with school counselors, could benefit from more specific knowledge about what counselors do and how they can work together. This book offers practical suggestions to those working in and out of schools to make those relationships more productive.

As a school counselor at heart, I hope that this book speaks to those in the school counseling community who are responsible for developing, managing, and delivering school counseling services and supports. It aims to provide framing and specific strategies for how to advocate for their programs and their profession; how to make changes in their own schools and districts so that they can fulfill their and their students' potential rather than being relegated to managing student records and supervising lunch periods. Many of them reading this book may not be surprised by the suggestions I am making. However, I expect that the examples presented here will give school counselors the encouragement and guidance for successfully engaging others in collaborative practices and change.

For these ideas to work, we must first get clearer about what that role is and what it is not. I am often reminded that the general public does not have a clear understanding of what school counselors actually do. In fact, the field of school counseling has been on the defensive for quite some time, thanks to a combination of role confusion, some individuals' sour experiences with counselors, and negative media portrayals. Film and television depictions frequently present counselors as clueless, negligent, unhelpful, burned out, and even harmful. For example, in one movie I saw, the school counselor is too busy writing her novel during school hours to offer much help to her students. That portrayal may be humorous, but it doesn't reflect reality; most counselors have nearly overwhelming caseloads of hundreds, and I vividly remember many days when I couldn't find five minutes to eat lunch. Such depictions undermine counselors' effectiveness by creating low expectations that deter students, families, and educational partners and leaders from leveraging all that school counselors have to offer. To remedy this problem, a new approach for school counseling should include intentional efforts to reach out to the entertainment, news, and policy communities to explain the true value of our role.

My hope is that by galvanizing many stakeholders around a shared understanding of school counseling and a framework to enact that understanding, we can become more effective and communicate that effectiveness to students, their families, and the general public. For all readers, this book outlines a path forward. It is a reminder of what is possible for counselors and, more importantly, their students.

SHIFTING PERSPECTIVES

Each academic year, I teach a group of smart young professionals eager to engage in school counseling work. Many of my students have found their way to the profession because they are most engaged when working with young people, are passionate about education, and see counseling as a good vehicle to promote social justice and better educational outcomes for students. Yet, when my students leave the program and begin their work in schools, they encounter school systems that reveal a profession in crisis. Many find themselves in situations like Alyssa's:

Alyssa was thrilled to be hired for her dream job as a high school counselor in her first year out of graduate school. She had looked forward to this day ever since her junior year in college, when she had shadowed a school counselor and immediately realized she had found her perfect career. As she began her new position, she was especially excited to be working with the innovative school leader who had recently restructured the school and adopted a focus on supporting the "whole child." She was eager to collaborate with teachers, use data to identify students' risk levels, run groups, and manage other responsibilities necessary to fulfill the school's mission. With her graduate training, she was ready to provide whatever academic, social emotional, and postsecondary supports were needed to set up students for success. Moreover, because the school was located in a small city with many youth programs, she was excited to learn more about them so that she could find ways to bridge students' school and community lives.

By November, however, Alyssa's excitement fizzled. She was frustrated by her job and wondering if she had made a mistake in choosing this path. She found herself spending inordinate amounts of time proctoring tests, covering the tardy desk, and writing up students who had been kicked out of class—and spending hardly any time on the social emotional and cognitive skill building she had prepared for. Why wasn't she included in her school's focus on the whole child, she wondered. Worse, some of the school's structures and policies seemed to directly undermine her role. For example, one school policy limited counselors from taking students out of classes. "How are we supposed to find out why students are struggling?" she asked at one staff meeting. The shrugs and eye rolls from her counseling colleagues suggested her concern was nothing new.

Alyssa couldn't quite figure out how the school would fulfill its mission to support the whole child when the professionals who knew most about development were struggling to do their jobs. Even worse, she knew that many students were grappling with major challenges, and if she didn't find a way to make changes in her work, those students would suffer the most.

Counselors like Alyssa are keenly aware that their good intentions and training are simply not enough, but many are not quite able to pinpoint why. Counselors are often implicated when reports show gaps in college enrollment, increased bullying behavior, and students lacking study skills. Yet, increased numbers of school shootings and demands on schools to more effectively screen for mental health needs have led many politicians to call for the hiring of more school counselors. In fact, in a recent survey of district leaders regarding how they intend to use Student Support and Academic Enrichment grant funds from the federally funded Every Student Succeeds Act (ESSA), respondents ranked school counseling as the second most common planned investment.[4] Yet, even if school counselors have the skills to screen students and provide personal supports, many are struggling to use all that they know to give students and schools the supports they require. Therefore, investments in new counselors need to be matched by renewed attention to the role.

One of the major reasons for this gap is that schools need a more strategic and systemic role for counselors. Despite the fact that almost 130,000 educational, guidance, school, and vocational counselors are employed in American schools—making them the second largest group of educators after teachers—few leaders know what they are positioned to do.[5] When the school counseling role is well articulated and supported, schools and students benefit. This was the case for Maria, one of Alyssa's classmates from graduate school:

In her first year out of graduate school, Maria was hired by a veteran principal of an urban high school who fundamentally believed that students who came to school having experienced trauma and other conditions related to poverty were not likely to thrive in school without adequate supports. This principal also believed that the school was responsible for preparing students for careers and, because he felt accountable for these aspects of students' development, was committed to supporting a team of school counselors. Before Maria's hiring, this principal worked collaboratively with the district's director of school counseling to hire two new school counselors and charged the entire department with developing a mission statement for the school.

Within her first year, Maria was tasked with setting up an intervention team, which would ultimately become a high-functioning support team that regularly used data to identify students' risk levels and connect them to appropriate supports. Maria enjoyed her new role, especially working alongside the other three school counselors who had many years of experience and mentored her at various points throughout the year.

In particular, one of her mentor counselors shared the district's early college awareness curriculum that was designed to be cotaught with a ninth-grade teacher. At first, Maria was reluctant to collaborate with teachers, having never been a classroom teacher herself. However, she quickly realized that the school had a culture of collaboration and the ninth-grade teachers saw the counselors as partners. Together, she and a team of teachers implemented the curriculum during Maria's first year. When the year ended, she used a survey created by the district to assess students' growth. To her surprise, 79 percent of the students reported increased awareness of postsecondary options, and 93 percent of the students could identify how their current classwork connected to their future goals. By the end of her first year, Maria felt good knowing that she could see the impact of her work and share it with the school principal.

The contrast between these stories, created as a composite from my students' experiences, is striking and reflective of the variation in school counseling that exists today. On the one hand, this variation is troubling; often, the school counseling role is poorly understood and underutilized. But on the other hand, it shows that creating systemic and successful roles for counselors is possible and suggests that some schools and districts offer models from which others can learn and grow.

Creating the conditions for school counselors to be most effective, however, will require tackling the systemic barriers that have made it extremely difficult for school counselors to perform their counseling roles as they were once envisioned. The reasons for this are as multifaceted as the role itself. Most notably, counselors' caseloads are unreasonably high to the point of compromising their ability to do their jobs. Although the American School Counselor Association recommends a caseload of 250 students to 1 counselor, the national average is 443:1.[6] Currently, Arizona and California rank among the highest with 903:1 and 708:1, respectively.[7] These data mean that in Arizona, *the average student has to compete with almost one thousand other students for time with a counselor.* With these caseloads, simply not enough counselors are available to provide the kinds of personalized supports that students need, and that is having real consequences for young people. For example, studies show that lower caseloads are associated with increases in student attendance, decreases in the need for disciplinary actions, and increases in four-year college-going rates.[8] As a result, some states such as New York have begun to take steps to lower extremely large caseloads.

Simply adding more counselors will address only part of the problem. Because superintendents and principals are often unaware of school counselors' skills and potential contributions, counselors do not routinely receive professional feedback or training to improve and are often assigned tasks simply to pick up the slack, such as managing schedules, proctoring exams, or monitoring lunch duty. I often hear from school counselors who implement innovative programming that they are succeeding not because of district support but in spite of it. Sometimes counseling departments don't even appear on a district's organizational chart. It is hard to imagine how counselors and school leaders can envision or implement a counseling program aligned with a school mission when their organizational relationship lacks clarity.

Forces outside of schools also contribute to a system in need of reform. Preservice pathways and professional development programs are inadequately preparing school counselors for the demands of their jobs. For example, many critics have pointed to the fact that graduate programs in school counseling overemphasize the clinical aspects of training with little attention to the aspects of college counseling, such as fostering early aspirations, engaging families in the process, and developing skills for postsecondary transitions.[9] My own research has found that school counselors in training rarely receive coursework in college- and career-readiness counseling, thereby making it difficult for counselors to engage in that aspect of their work. In a similar vein, school administrators don't receive preparation or information during their graduate training regarding the role of counselors. This lack of knowledge certainly makes it hard for counselors to receive adequate supervision and guidance from their school leaders, who are typically responsible for evaluating them and defining how they spend their time.

One result of all these challenges is the arrival of a constellation of out-of-school programs and partnerships, staffed by people ready to step in and fill the gaps. With dwindling budgets and competing demands for funds, many schools have begun to rely on college access programs, social service agencies, and community youth programs to provide specialized supports that enhance school programming. These programs are well intentioned and sometimes effective but can lead to fragmentation. Counselors tell me that they find themselves handing over the work they were trained to do and which drew them to the profession so that they have time for the administrative and clerical tasks that are distracting them from their core work. At best, these programs relieve schools of the overwhelming needs brought by students, such as counseling and college planning. But at worst, they exacerbate deficiencies in the school counseling system because they keep school leaders and external partners from looking at the factors that contribute to counselors' full plates in the first place. When I recently proposed to the president of a private foundation that he invest in training for school counselors as part of his foundation's efforts to increase college-going rates, he was quick to dismiss the idea because, he said, "The schools just waste the money, and the counselors are terrible." I knew this was a gross mischaracterization and a missed opportunity; I also knew it would take more than one conversation to change his—and many others'—assessment of the profession.

A TIME FOR CHANGE

School counselors can serve students more effectively—and they want to. They also know that their school and district leaders want the same thing. Now is the ideal time to refocus and reenvision the role of school counselors, thanks to four major trends in education that are opening a window of opportunity for change.

First, superintendents, philanthropists, politicians, and business leaders have all called for more attention to postsecondary preparation and success. They have become increasingly aware of the large gaps in this area between more and less advantaged students, and as a result, schools have stepped up their responsibility for students' success in college, career, and life. For example, Chicago Mayor Rahm Emanuel proposed a policy requiring seniors to show evidence of a postsecondary plan (such as a job offer or college acceptance) in order to graduate. Placing more responsibility on schools to raise the standards for students is a good thing, especially in tandem with other district efforts to close opportunity gaps between more and less advantaged students. School counselors are well suited to consider how to implement such a policy in a way that will ensure all students are set up to meet the requirement, along with community and university-based partners who might share responsibility for helping students meet a new graduation requirement of this type.

Imagine a school where school counselors embed this requirement into classroom-based lessons beginning in grade nine and use data to track students' progress toward meeting the postsecondary plan goal with input and support from community partners. Such a systemic approach is far more likely to lead to success than a last-minute scramble to help students put plans into place.

Second, educators, parents, and policy makers are becoming aware of the importance of social emotional learning (SEL) and the development of "noncognitive" skills.[10] Counselors are often the only people in schools with training in developmental psychology and are well positioned to support such efforts. In some schools, the counseling role includes leading advisories, facilitating classroom-based social emotional curricula, and guiding Positive Behavioral Intervention and Supports (PBIS) systems.[11] Emily Goodman-Scott, a counselor-educator who has written extensively on the alignment between school counseling and PBIS, argues that school counselors, because of their training in prevention, counseling, and advocacy, are uniquely positioned to coordinate the implementation of PBIS programs and collaborate with PBIS teams to identify appropriate interventions.[12] Imagine a school where the school counselors are routinely leading prevention curricula and group counseling to promote a positive school climate through social skill development. School counselors' involvement in SEL could be more widespread, and the field is ripe for learning from the promising practices in schools at the leading edge of this movement. Universal support for social emotional skills will require that counselors expand their prevention efforts and provide consultation to teachers and school staff.[13] Maurice Elias, a psychology professor and leading expert in SEL, contends that school counselors play a pivotal role in promoting students' social emotional development. Elias points out, however, that although counselors should be seen as the "quarterback of the team," they are seen as positions worth cutting when budgets are tight.[14]

Third, in addition to promoting college and career readiness and social emotional skills, counselors also have the potential to fill gaping

holes in school-based mental health. In the wake of high-profile tragedies including suicides and school shootings, communities have questioned the limited availability of mental health supports in schools. For
example, a report published in response to the devastating school shooting in Newtown, Connecticut, blamed local schools for not monitoring shooter Adam Lanza's emotional and academic progress, pointing to
poorly trained staff and a lack of resources. Although it is logical to call
on school counselors to screen for mental health needs, provide support
as needed, and make referrals to social service agencies, research suggests that they are only minimally involved. Surveys of school counselors report that although they believe their role should include supporting
students' mental health needs, they rarely have time or support to engage
in that work.[15] Imagine a school where the school counselors ensure that
all students are screened and treated for mental health needs, teachers
receive consultation and support for how to support students, and social
service agencies have clear systems for receiving referrals and maintaining ongoing communication with schools. Importantly, imagine a school
where counselors have enough time to build relationships with students
so that students feel safe disclosing emerging symptoms and struggles.

Finally, the academic standards movement, which shapes our current
educational climate, hinges on counselors helping all students to meet
high achievement standards. Certainly, the standards movement, with an
emphasis on raising expectations for all students, has made progress in
getting the majority of students to perform at a high level.[16] However,
those subgroups of students for whom we have not witnessed such progress would benefit from counseling to identify what stands in the way of
their educational progress. For this struggling group, academic instruction and preparation alone are often insufficient. Rather, this lowest performing group of students will require counselors who can attend to the
issues that otherwise interfere with their school engagement and achievement. Studies show that counselors can be effective in helping students
improve their organizational, time management, and study skills.[17] Imagine a school district where school counselors regularly use data to iden-

tify which students warrant intensive targeted supports, conduct home visits for those students with chronic absenteeism, and identify alternative programs when necessary.[18]

Instead of focusing blame on school counselors, as recent reports on college and career readiness, mental health, and academic achievement have done, the current moment can be a time for focusing resources on a profession that is well positioned to meet key student needs.[19] We have known for some time that students are facing a considerably different educational context than in the past, and many preparation programs for teachers and school leaders are undergoing reform to these changes, such as the increased number of students experiencing trauma. The time is ripe for school counselor training to make those changes, too.

From the White House to private philanthropy, policy windows have begun to open to galvanize the profession. Counselors themselves are poised and ready for change. In 2014, First Lady Michelle Obama launched Reach Higher, an initiative to promote college access and success among low-income students. Along with a focus on raising students' postsecondary aspirations and understanding financial aid, this initiative included a primary focus on supporting school counselors and the school counseling profession. Speaking at the national ASCA conference, hosting School Counselor of the Year awards at the White House, and speaking to counselors in her final address to the nation, Michelle Obama raised public awareness about the importance of this profession to student success. The groundswell of interest evident in response to this initiative is a testament to the desire among many in education for change.

Until now, however, change has been slow for the professional school counseling community. The reason is in part that reform in school counseling has largely reached only those in the field. Organizations such as the American School Counselor Association (ASCA) and the National Association for College Admission Counseling (NACAC) provide important leadership and professional development for those working as school counselors; however, these efforts have barely scratched the surface in changing the systems in which counselors work. For example, NACAC has produced persuasive research that has led to improvements being made in school counseling training programs; however, school leaders' understanding of counselors' skills and knowledge remains low. Likewise, although ASCA has long advocated for counselors' work to span academic, social emotional, and postsecondary development, some educators and leaders continue to hold low expectations of counselors' ability to work in all three areas.

This slow rate of change hurts all students, though some more than others. Recent events have called attention to the fact that some students, especially students of color and those from low-income communities, have limited access to school-based counselors. According to the Office of Civil Rights at the US Department of Education, "1.6 million students attend a school with a sworn law enforcement officer but not a school counselor."[20] Perhaps most alarming, counselors in schools serving high percentages of low-income students have the largest caseloads, despite the fact that their students are most in need of their services, from coping with the mental health consequences of trauma to navigating an unfamiliar world of postsecondary planning.[21] Some studies show that counselors working in schools with low college-going rates spend less time devoted to college counseling than those who work in high schools with high college-going rates.[22] This difference in the amount of time counselors dedicate to college planning has the potential to disproportionately impact some students more than others.

The stakes are higher in low-income communities, where the effects of poverty are significant and the safety nets are fewer. All kids need support, however, and all communities would benefit from improvements in school counseling. While some students would benefit from support to manage a stressful situation at home, others need assistance with strategies to handle a dilemma with a teacher or peer. Thus, a new approach that calls on districts and school leaders to attend to the system has the potential to ensure equal access to much-needed supports.

School leaders want those supports and so do parents. A recent poll by *Phi Delta Kappan* found that Americans expect schools to do more than provide academic instruction.[23] They expect schools to prepare students for careers and also to support students' development of interpersonal skills such as cooperating, solving problems, and showing respect for others. Likewise, parents overwhelmingly want schools to provide mental health supports to those who need it. Yet, meeting those expectations successfully depends on a clear understanding of how the current system may not yet be well set up to meet these goals and what we can do better.

FROM CHALLENGES TO OPPORTUNITIES

This book is, at its heart, about student opportunity, but it is deeply informed by my own professional pathway and experiences. Professionals across many industries talk about the spark that incited them to pursue a career in medicine or the arts or business. For me, it was my high school counselor, Miss Miskie. Before I met her, I was primed to be a teacher. My mother was a teacher, and when I was growing up, I played a lot of "school," with a chalkboard and many dolls. But I was always more interested in what my dolls wished to be when they grew up than I was in helping them master addition. In time, I came to be so interested in counseling that Miss Miskie invited me to be a "guidance assistant" in her office, and I eventually got my own office as a licensed school counselor in a Boston public high school. The list of what I loved about my work was long and included amazing students and families, teacher and counseling colleagues who affirmed my path in education, and the ability to work with young people in a school setting. My official focus was college and career counseling, but as I told an author who interviewed me about my job, "in a school with kids who have many needs, you end up doing much more." I loved the additional counseling I provided and never shied away from new things.

It took me five years to realize that my do-it-all approach wasn't working. I encountered many unexpected frustrations: My caseload was too high; I lacked some of the training to do my job well; I spent too much time on administrative tasks; I had colleagues who did not share my desire to expand the role; I rarely received supervision or critical feedback; and I never had enough time to do all the things on my list. I felt I was regularly putting Band-Aids on problems rather than addressing the underlying causes. I watched too many students who had gone off to college return each spring, having left school for academic, social, or financial reasons. I wondered whether I gave those students the time and care they needed to find the right path. Would some of those students have benefitted from counseling earlier in their educational careers? I eventually realized that, even with the best of intentions and the support of a principal who fundamentally believed in the power of counseling services, I wasn't able to give the students everything they needed.

Years later, as a counselor educator and researcher, I realized that I was not part of an extended school counseling program and, as such, had been missing a clear set of standards to drive my work and professional development programs to help me meet those standards. Although I worked with numerous valuable partners, I never felt that, together, we created a coherent system. Instead, it was more of a catch-as-catch-can model.

Now that I am the director of a counseling education program, my graduate students sometimes argue that the model in which we are training them is too idealistic and does not necessarily reflect the reality of the conditions for the profession today. Indeed, we need to revise our training approaches, but we also need to change the role of school counselors and the systems in which they work in American education. Today, we are better prepared than ever before to make those changes. We have not seen an opportunity like this since the post-*Sputnik* moment in the 1950s, when concerns about America's global competitiveness led politicians to see school counselors as vital for guiding students to science careers. To seize this moment, we need to articulate the challenges our schools are facing . . . and what we can do to help.

BRIGHT SPOTS

In this book, I call attention to the high expectations we can and should set for all school counselors, along with the requisite professional working conditions and supports necessary for them to meet those expectations. To meet new demands placed on schools, we need models illustrating where counselors have been successful when conditions have been ripe for them to succeed. Thus, I offer examples of counselors, schools, districts, and even states that have experimented with new models and structures and have found that changes in expectations of counselors, revisions to their roles, and investments in positions and programming lead to improvements in student outcomes and school climate.

School districts and schools cannot do this work alone, however. For this reason, this book also calls on the policy and philanthropic communities to examine their current investments in school counseling. Although private philanthropy has drastically increased its investments in educational endeavors such as nonprofit programs and charter schools, parallel investments in school counseling are nascent. Likewise, major differences in statewide policies regarding mandated school counseling programs and related support call into question whether all students across the nation have equal access to high-quality counseling supports. By highlighting states and funders that have taken important steps toward equalizing opportunity through school counseling reform, I provide examples we can all learn from.

A ROADMAP FOR THIS BOOK

The organization of this book is designed to offer a new way of conceptualizing school counseling and present options for actualizing this new approach that will enable a more strategic, efficient, and effective role for school counselors. The first chapter describes the context of school counseling, offering a basic history of the profession, specific historical trends and events that have shaped the field, and how such an evolution has contributed to the multifaceted and ambiguous nature of the school counselor's role today. Chapter 2 presents a new approach to school counseling that elevates the centrality of the school counselor role and portrays counselors playing a role in education much like primary care physicians play in health care—forming strong relationships with students, providing some direct services, and then referring students to specialists and partners and ensuring continuity across services. Chapter 3 highlights the strong network of specialized supports provided by teachers, community partners, and students and how counselors can best leverage these important assets. Chapter 4 defines how school leaders can support this new approach by creating the conditions that are necessary for counselors to positively influence students' educational experiences such as counselor assignments and responsibilities. Chapter 5 explains the role that district leaders can play in supporting school-level change through role articulation, hiring practices, licensure and training needs, and evaluation systems that create a strong professional experience for counselors. Chapter 6 highlights private philanthropy and how new investments in system-level changes in school counseling have the potential to address a range of pressing issues in schools. This chapter also considers important shifts in policy, such as mandating that schools have school counseling programs and establishing maximum student-to-counselor caseloads that are essential to counselor effectiveness. In the concluding chapter, I sum up the urgent need for a new way of thinking about school counseling and its potential impact for all students, but especially traditionally underserved students.

Throughout this book, I present examples that highlight the challenges and opportunities that schools and school counselors are experiencing. Most of these examples depict exciting work taking place in schools and districts, and thus, both are named. In other parts of the book, I share stories that reflect composites drawn from a broad range of my professional experiences; in these cases, I use only a first name to distinguish these composites from real-world examples.

A NOTE ABOUT TERMS

Throughout the book, I use the term *school counselor* rather than the more well-known term *guidance counselor*. My usage is not solely based on the fact that being referred to as a guidance counselor grates on many counselors. While it is true that this irritation has prompted many counselors to correct their well-meaning colleagues and even sport T-shirts with *Guidance* crossed out in exchange for *SCHOOL COUNSELOR*, counselors' preference for correct terminology is not merely a trendy move. Counselors have consciously shifted away from the term *guidance*, which reflects the historical emphasis on vocational guidance, to better illustrate the professional scope of their role today. The term *guidance counselor* was initially coined in the early 1900s to refer to teachers who took on additional responsibilities providing vocational guidance to students. Yet that was over one hundred years ago, and the role has changed too much to rely on an outdated term. Today, counselors' work involves many aspects of a complex educational system and multiple dimensions of students' development. Thus, *guidance* belittles the profession in ways that do not serve students well. It narrows the scope of counselors' work and programming, thus misrepresenting their actual contributions to student success.

This shift in terminology mimics other changes in educational staff titles, such as *home economics*. Indeed, schools today hire *family and consumer science* educators, who teach courses similar to what was once understood as *home ec*. Likewise, what was once known as *vocational education* is now known as *career and technical education*. Similar to school counseling, these shifts in terms were intentional and have been accompanied by changes in instructional content and professional training. A similar evolution has occurred for counselors. Whereas school counselors lead classroom lessons that support students' future goals, that is only one aspect of their role. They also use data to identify students at risk of dropping out, refer students for intensive mental health support and treatment, implement positive behavioral support programs, screen students for signs of suicide, and perform a host of other responsibilities that extend well beyond career development. That is, changes in the role have brought about comprehensive school counseling programs that are designed to support school culture and mission instead of focusing solely on delivering services to students.

To continue to use the term *guidance* is outdated, and it is misleading. Fortunately, this change is easy, free, and, I believe, matters a lot. In this book, I stick to the term *school counselor* unless using direct quotes or sharing the history of the profession.

A NEW DAY

Today more focus than ever before is placed on ensuring that all students, regardless of background, receive a strong education that prepares them for their future in a twenty-first-century economy. Achieving this goal absolutely depends on our willingness to address the systemic challenges that limit school counselors' contributions in schools. There is no better time to take on this challenge because educators are looking for new solutions and strategies to solve pressing issues such as gaps in academic achievement and increased mental health needs. The field of education desperately needs a change in how schools think about and employ their school counselors. Counselors are ready and eager to be a part of that change.

1

THE PAST AS PROLOGUE

*Moving from Vocational Guidance to Comprehensive
Student Support*

[A] tendency dangerous to the cause of vocational guidance is the tendency to load the vocational counselor with so many duties foreign to the office that little real counseling can be done. The principal, and often the counselor himself, has a very indefinite idea of the proper duties of this new office. The counselor's time is more free from definite assignments with groups or classes of pupils than is that of the ordinary teacher. If well-chosen he has administrative ability. It is perfectly natural, therefore, for the principal to assign one administrative duty after another to the counselor until he becomes practically assistant principal, with little time for the real work of a counselor.

—George Myers, 1923[1]

Although its language reflects a different time, I imagine many school counselors reading the preceding quote believe the same could be said about today's counselors. Yet, in 1923, when George Myers, a leading advocate of vocational guidance, made this statement, he was offering a warning to educators: if not monitored closely, the work of the counselor could drift far from actual counseling.

It is nearly impossible to capture the range of things that school counselors do in a single day to support students' academic, social emotional, and postsecondary development, but this was not always the case. Since the inception of this position, the role and function of school counseling have shifted and expanded as changing societal trends have placed new demands on schools. Historical trends and events, such as immigration and the growing importance of a postsecondary credential, have gradually contributed to the current multifaceted and ambiguous nature of the school counselor's role.[2] Whereas school counselors were once focused solely on supporting students' vocational development, counselors began to take on responsibilities in other areas, particularly mental health, academic intervention and support, and college counseling.

Most school counselors today report wanting to spend more time supporting students' academic success and healthy development and less time on administrative tasks, suggesting that these early warnings from Myers still hold today. How has the evolution of this profession transpired so that counselors today report spending too much of their time on noncounseling duties such as test proctoring and scheduling?[3] Given the unique positions counselors hold and the potential to address many of the key issues facing schools, why is it that counselors struggle to do their jobs effectively? Why do so many reports define counselors as the weak link in schools rather than part of the solution? This chapter examines how the answers to those questions are embedded in the history of the profession and how we can build on that history to move forward.

In this chapter, I describe the evolution of school counseling and how the multiple dimensions of the job have complicated counselors' ability to deliver the quality supports students need in today's context. With attention to key historical shifts, I present how new demands placed on schools ultimately increased expectations of school counselors with little additional support. This chapter further argues how placing counselors in a central role to support students, with collaboration from in- and out-of-school partners, holds great promise for the current state of schools.

PROVIDING VOCATIONAL GUIDANCE: THE BEGINNING OF SCHOOL COUNSELING

Counselors' earliest roles in schools began with a focus on career development or, as it was referred to at the time, *vocational guidance*. During the Progressive Era of the late nineteenth and early twentieth centuries, schools maintained a strong focus on ensuring that youth not only received an adequate education but also had the skills to ultimately secure gainful employment and contribute to society. Vocational guidance became an important service that schools provided, thanks in large part to Frank Parsons, a noted education and social reformer who is considered the father of the movement. At the turn of the twentieth century, Parsons worked in settlement houses and other community settings, driven by the belief that vocational choice was of utmost importance to achieving individual and social efficiency, and that youth especially needed adequate guidance to choose a vocation best suited to their skill set and interests. While many counselors may not know Parsons by name, they are sure to be familiar with his trait and factor theory, which is the basis for many career interest inventories that counselors use with students today.[4] At its core, this concept describes a process that includes helping students understand themselves and then matching their passions and strengths to the world of work. Counselors today lead "Who am I" activities and utilize strength-finder tools; then they expose students to events that present a wide array of occupational options to which they can match their strengths. From elementary to high schools, school counselors use Parsons's early work to guide their work with students.

Teachers were the first professionals to perform vocational guidance in schools. These educators, with no formal training, were named *guidance counselors*. In 1917, the federal government began supporting the vocational guidance movement, initially with $7.2 million to compensate teachers and set up state boards in charge of vocational education.[5] By 1946, annual appropriations for vocational education had grown to $29 million, and federal funding allowed for advancements in research, training programs, and salaries.[6] With additional funding and growing responsibilities, schools began to hire specifically trained counselors to perform vocational guidance duties. Likewise, training programs with a focus on vocational guidance began to take hold.

Today, school counselors continue to play a key role in students' career development. Although high school counselors place more emphasis on college than career since a "college for all" vision has become commonplace, counselors do support career development by hosting career days, disseminating career interest inventories, exposing students to careers in specific industries such as science, technology, engineering, and math (STEM), and connecting students to career-oriented enrichment programs. In their book *Learning for Careers*, my colleagues Nancy Hoffman and Bob Schwartz call attention to many states that have looked more broadly than the "college for all" philosophy and successfully swayed employers to create direct pathways to the labor market from high school. As is evident in Hoffman and Schwartz's related Pathways to Prosperity initiative, policy makers and leading educators are starting to call for more applied learning that links school experiences to future career options through work-based education and apprenticeships. Career and technical education, known today as CTE, is experiencing a resurgence. School counselors, armed with training in career development, are uniquely positioned to support CTE programs. In states such as Missouri, Nebraska, and Utah, collaborations between comprehensive school counseling programs and career and technical education programs have given way to integrated programming, shared resources, and professional development.[7]

With a strong history in vocational development, counselors continue to serve their original purpose through their current engagement in career readiness and development. Although the labor market trends and forces are quite different, students today continue to rely on counselors to bring career development programming into schools, classrooms, and programming.

DELIVERING SOCIAL EMOTIONAL SUPPORT

By the early 1930s, the guidance field had grown beyond vocational guidance, due to the shifting populace and advances in counseling psychology.

The 1940s saw an increasing emphasis on social, emotional, and personal aspects of counseling to ensure that students were well adjusted in all aspects of their lives. This interest was partially driven by waves of immigration to the United States, which created a desire to acculturate new members of the American society. Demands for more personal counseling were also spurred on by burgeoning attention to mental health and the introduction of psychological measurement. This focus ultimately became known as *pupil-personnel services*. Its impact on school counselors' roles was captured by psychologist Charles Gilbert Wrenn in his groundbreaking 1963 book, *The Counselor in a Changing World*, which argued that counselors should commit two-thirds to three-fourths of their time to individual therapeutic counseling and consulting with educational colleagues and students' families about student mental health. Initially, the mental health function focused on addressing problems, but as the field of psychology gradually shifted toward preventing problems and fostering healthy development, counselors' roles shifted again. This shift had implications for the scope and scale of counselors' work, as it brought about programs to promote all children's mental health as opposed to focusing on a small number of children with acute problems. This focus on promotion widened the scope of whom school counselors served and how. With this commitment to providing mental health support came a realization that specialized training, distinct from that of teachers, was in order. Thus, the expansion of the role was accompanied by the formalization of counselor training programs.

As we know, students today continue to need personal, social, and emotional supports to succeed at school and in life, and this domain remains a significant component of school counselors' current array of responsibilities. In fact, in recent years researchers and policy makers have begun to recognize the importance of such supports. In this realm, school counseling today touches on a wide range of topics such as identity development, social skill development, relationship support, family and individual stress management, and ways of coping with specific stressors such as homelessness.

Of course, the kinds of challenges counselors face today differ from those in the 1940s or even the 1990s. For example, providing support to transgender and gender-nonconforming students and running a classroom lesson on appropriate social media usage reflect issues that were not even recognized or existent twenty years ago. Counselors are also increasingly called on to deal with crises. Unfortunately, tragedies such as student deaths, natural disasters, community violence, mass shootings, and events in the media such as the shooting of unarmed black men have created the need for support for traumatized students and staff, as well as communitywide responses to restore school safety. Even with this wide and deep range of needs, studies show that school counseling programs are having an impact on students' social emotional adjustment. Findings include improved attendance, lower discipline rates, improved attitudes about school, a sense of belonging, and reduced referrals to special education.[8]

Mounting Mental Health Concerns

In today's context, school counselors have also been called on to direct even more of their time toward mental health issues. Researchers estimate that between 13 and 20 percent of children under the age of eighteen experience mental, emotional, or behavioral challenges, all of which may impact students' educational achievement and attainment; therefore, addressing such problems can enhance student performance.[9] Students of color, who are often low income and impacted by the effects of poverty, are also significantly more likely to experience anxiety and mood disorders.[10] Likewise, new studies have found that schools with a high percentage of students from affluent communities are reporting high levels of substance abuse, depression, and anxiety.[11] Each of these trends has brought about a new set of expectations for counselors to support struggling students.

At present, schools are increasingly being asked to address these growing mental health and wellness challenges. Because a large majority of mental health disorders are diagnosed before the age of eighteen, school counselors and teachers use early identification and screenings to identify concerns. In addition, counselors' current practices to address mental health include facilitating group counseling sessions for selected groups of students; promoting positive health behaviors; referring students to mental health professionals in the community; and educating teachers, staff, and families about how to identify students who may be experiencing mental health issues and other stressors that compromise students' well-being.[12]

Recent increases in bullying, student suicides, and mass shootings have led school counselors to expand their programs to address social, emotional, and prosocial skills. For example, many counselors today have implemented bullying interventions to reduce the victimization that some students experience in schools, while also leading schoolwide efforts to create inclusive and safe school communities. However, schools are also expected to identify, support, and sometimes refer to appropriate services those students with mental health needs. As a result, many school counselors use universal screening as a Tier 1 support to identify those students for specialized mental health counseling.

Anne Erickson, a nationally board-certified school counselor from Minnesota, implemented depression and anxiety screenings and a suicide awareness program at her high school to reduce the risk of depression and suicidal thoughts among the student body.[13] As part of the intervention, parents of students at risk for depression receive information from the school counselor about relevant mental health resources, including local medical providers. In the seventeen years since the start of the program, the percentage of students with depressive symptoms has dropped dramatically. Since the program started, the school has had one suicide; however, neither that student nor his peers had experienced the screening or education program. A secondary benefit of the program, the school has also observed students talking more openly about mental health and an increase in the number of students who seek help directly from the school's counselors. This example highlights the unique role that counselors have begun to play in preventing and responding to emerging student needs.

With the increasing threat of school violence and mass school shootings, many politicians have called for more school counselors and social workers in schools. Certainly, counselors are not a replacement for significant policy limits to the accessibility of weapons. However, having counselors in place to identify students in need of mental health supports is the best response to safety concerns, and thus, communities have added this safety role to counselors' job descriptions.

As counselors address social emotional needs, many of them also need to work hand in hand with social workers, whose profession was established in community settings but was later integrated into schools. School social workers initially tracked attendance issues, performed psychological testing, and connected families and schools, but their role has grown to incorporate therapy and other mental health services.

Some have suggested that school counselors and social workers should have separate roles with clear boundaries—academic issues and mental health, respectively—but in reality, these domains have significant overlap. Students' academic issues are often inseparable from social and personal challenges, as I often saw when I was counseling students about absenteeism and learned that they were homeless or had a mentally ill family member. In many cases, school counselors emphasize *more* school-oriented issues and social workers take on issues outside of school, but these professionals must work together. Similarly, many schools partner with social service agencies to provide in-school therapy, but to be successful, schools need someone to connect the pieces smoothly and efficiently.

Mounting concerns about mental health and school safety, along with present-day student concerns, illustrate just how much the school counseling role has grown. In addition to the original purpose of vocational counseling, the added layer of social emotional counseling has further extended the profession.

PROMOTING COLLEGE AND CAREER READINESS

Helping students plan for their futures has long been a part of the counselor role, but the current emphasis on college readiness has increased demands on counselors. Most recently, the decrease in entry-level positions that do not require a college degree has shaped this third layer of counselors' responsibilities—college counseling. As a result, educational leaders have begun to use college enrollment as a barometer for educational opportunity, particularly in the face of glaring gaps in college enrollment between students of color and their white counterparts. Researchers began to document that students from low-income communities had far less access to college preparation supports than their peers from middle and upper class communities in the 1990s. Exacerbating this issue was the fact that students from low-income communities were further disadvantaged by lacking some forms of postsecondary planning support from families who had not gone through the process. At the same time, new reports and studies began to highlight the experiences of students who had not received support from their counselor, suggesting that some counselors act as gatekeepers to postsecondary opportunity rather than facilitators of access and enrollment.[14] This criticism that counselors were tracking some students into college and others into careers pushed many counselors to adopt a universal "college for all" philosophy. Counselors began to reduce their involvement in helping individual students decide where to apply and matriculate and to refocus their resources on promoting college awareness and readiness for everyone. That shift is reflected in the movement for early college awareness, spurred by a 1987 report by the College Board that called for counseling programs to begin preparing students early for the postsecondary transition process so they would all be ready.[15] This expansion into college counseling added yet another layer to the scope of school counselors' role. No longer limited to planning support for high school juniors and seniors, counselors' engagement in college counseling began to start earlier and even included school-level interventions such as implementing "college week" or inviting school alumni to speak to current students about their experiences with higher education.

Another major shift that extended school counselors' focus on college counseling was the impact of the Obama presidency on education. Increasing college completion rates in the United States was a major initiative of the Obama administration. During a joint session of Congress in 2009, President Obama set forth a goal for the country to have the highest proportion of college graduates by the year 2020.[16] In 2014, First Lady Michelle Obama launched the Reach Higher initiative in support of President Obama's 2020 "North Star" goal of increasing the number of Americans completing postsecondary education. In addition to engaging with students directly in order to boost their college enrollment and completion rates, the initiative put a spotlight on supporting high school counselors who advise these students as they consider their postsecondary options.[17] As noted in the 2017 *Reach Higher Progress Report*, "this initiative marked the first time a national leader called for improvements to the school counseling profession, with a specific focus on college readiness counseling."[18] This initiative was a clarion call for supporting school counseling as a mechanism to promote college readiness.

College counseling responsibilities have continued to swell in response to new research and support from national organizations, including the College Board; the National Association for College Admission Counseling (NACAC), which has spelled out the competencies needed in the counselor role; and the National College Advising Network. Today, counselors at all levels are expected to be the primary producers of college counseling and support. Utilizing data from the US Department of Education's Educational Longitudinal Study of 2002, college planning expert Andrew Belasco found that students who reported speaking with a school counselor about college were, on average, significantly more likely to enroll in higher education, including at four-year institutions.[19] Interestingly, the outcomes of students from low-income backgrounds were the most positively affected by meeting with a school counselor. In addition, low-SES students who met with a counselor in both tenth and twelfth grade were more likely to enroll at a four-year institution compared to those who met with a counselor in only one grade. But it's not just high school counselors who matter for college. Elementary and middle school counselors are also expected to raise early college aspirations and help young children connect their schooling to their futures. A former mentor of mine, Janet Palmer-Owens, created Boston's first elementary college and career center at the Mason Elementary School. Counselors at that school regularly utilized the center's books for children about careers, brought students to the center to learn about college and see college banners and posters, and drew on resources to educate parents about opportunities for their children. Likewise, middle school counselors across the country deliver college preparation support when they encourage teachers to share their own postsecondary pathways or when they create clear middle to high school transition plans and programs.

As with social emotional support, the college counseling role is often supplemented by partnerships with other professionals, often strengthening resources for students but causing confusion or even exacerbating inequities. Nonprofit and community-based programs serve many low-income and first-generation college students. These programs began with federal TRIO programs such as Upward Bound, Talent Search, and Gaining Early Awareness Readiness for Undergraduate Education (GEAR UP). The programs provide important resources to students and, in some cases, have evidence of improved postsecondary outcomes.[20] However, as promising as these programs are, their reach is limited. During 2013–14, TRIO awarded 2,791 grants totaling $785,720,504 and reaching nearly 758,000 students across the country.[21] This number is small when considering that approximately 15 million students were enrolled in grades nine through twelve and 3,479,920 students graduated from high school in 2013–14. Because estimates indicate that nearly 40 percent of all public school students are identified as low income, the reach of these programs is limited.[22]

To provide concentrated college counseling supports, some schools have begun to hire specific college counselors to support students' postsecondary planning and transitions. For instance, many charter and independent schools hire specialized counselors to work intensively with students on the college planning process. In addition, some affluent families hire private counselors to assist students through the college application process, a trend that educational researcher Patricia McDonough has attributed to the combination of competitive college admissions and limited school-based college counseling programs.[23] This trend raises concerns about the inequity that exists when those with more resources receive intensive supports, whereas those with fewer resources must compete with hundreds of other students for similar college planning support. When school counselors are leveraged to work collaboratively with college counseling specialists, they can ensure all students have access to support and reduce confusion among who provides what services.

Their role in college counseling therefore continues to be a big part of high school counselors' jobs. In many ways, this responsibility fell in line with the original focus on vocational guidance; however, along with social emotional counseling, it further broadened the scope of their professional responsibilities.

SUPPORTING ACADEMIC ACHIEVEMENT

The most recent extension of counselors' role is embodied in the current articulation and alignment of counseling programs and academic achievement. For several decades, the better part of school counseling has been in service to academic achievement. For instance, supporting students' mental and emotional health in schools is, in part, intended to address factors that hinder student engagement and success in school. However, a broader educational reform movement created the context for counselors to become more explicit about their role in the academic domain. In 1994, the reauthorization of the Elementary and Secondary Education Act (ESEA) created the expectation that all states raise academic standards for all students. This legislation codified the standards-based movement at the federal level and ultimately influenced school counselors' roles also.

Even without clear guidance from federal policy, the school counseling profession joined the standards-based movement to promote rigorous academic expectations for all students. The leading school counseling profession, the American School Counselor Association (ASCA), encouraged counselors to embrace their part in supporting schoolwide change. In their 1994 brief, *The School Counselor's Role in Educational Reform*, ASCA called on counselors to become "partners in student achievement." This shift was captured in ASCA's refined definition of school counseling in the following way:

> Counseling is a process of helping people by assisting them in making decisions and changing behavior. School counselors work with all students, school staff, families, and members of the community as an integral part of the education program. School counseling programs promote school success through a focus on academic achievement, prevention, and intervention activities, advocacy, and social emotional and career development.[24]

This revised definition brought about changes in practice, greater clarity of role, and new directions for greater accountability to the profession. To begin with, the school counseling community began to articulate the links between counseling and making progress toward social justice and educational opportunity. The National Center for Transforming School Counseling (NCTSC), established in collaboration between the Education Trust and MetLife Foundation in 2003, played a critical role in advancing this movement. Based on their research on the status of school counseling at the time, NCTSC articulated a "new vision" for the school counseling profession in which counselors would serve as leaders, advocates, collaborators, and researchers.[25] Within these new roles, counselors were expected to use data to identify gaps in educational outcomes; provide leadership and direction to schools implementing academic interventions; and align their individual, group, and classroom work with clear standards.[26] The NCTSC is responsible for changes to counselor education programs and school counseling programs that continue to exist today.

More recently, the No Child Left Behind (NCLB) Act of 2001 aimed "to close the achievement gap with accountability, flexibility, and choice, so that no child is left behind."[27] This education reform bill reauthorizing the 1965 Elementary and Secondary Education Act was passed during the George W. Bush administration and was specifically focused on increasing the academic achievement of disadvantaged students as well as English language learners, improving the recruitment and training of school teachers and principals, expanding parental choice, and implementing accountability systems such as school and district "report cards" to assess quality. NCLB largely aligned with the ASCA model, especially with regard to the importance of accountability systems in developing effective schools and high-quality counseling programs.[28]

In particular, NCLB required school practices and reform interventions, including those related to school counseling, to be rooted in evidence-based research. This requirement spawned an evidence-based research movement in the counseling field. The evidence-based movement has origins in medicine, where there was a call for medical professionals to use existing research to guide their practices and to integrate new research-based knowledge with their clinical skills.[29] Thomas Sexton, formerly the Director of the Center for Adolescent and Family Studies and Professor Emeritus at Indiana University–Bloomington, was one of the leading voices in the late 1990s for the adoption of an evidence-based practice approach in the larger counseling field. He argued that the "artificial dichotomy between research and practice [is] not only irrelevant but also potentially harmful to the current and future status of counseling practice and preparation," as outcome research has the potential to not only strengthen counselor training and practices but also improve client outcomes.[30]

At a 2003 research summit of the American School Counselor Association (ASCA) and the Association for Counselor Education and Supervision (ACES), counseling leaders determined that an independent body was needed to conduct reviews of the school counseling evidence base, identify necessary research studies, and document alignment between school counseling practices and NCLB standards.[31] The National Panel for School Counseling Evidence-Based Practice was then organized that same year by the newly established Center for School Counseling Outcome Research and Evaluation (CSCORE) at the University of Massachusetts–Amherst. Ultimately, Carey Dimmitt, John Carey, and Trish Hatch built on the work of Sexton, articulating an evidenced-based practice (EBP) model built on three elements: (1) problem description, or knowing what needs to be addressed; (2) outcome research use, or drawing upon the research base to determine what is likely to work; and (3) intervention evaluation, or evaluating the effectiveness of the intervention.[32]

Nowadays, many school counselors are actively engaged in accountability practices driven by their desire to contribute to narrowing achievement gaps. These practices are supported by the profession's adoption of evidence-based school counseling practices that empower counselors to use data to guide their work and measure their programs' impact. Carey Dimmitt and John Carey, leaders in the EBP movement, describe this practice as using evidence to determine an exact problem, to identify an appropriate intervention or response, and then to examine the data to determine the effectiveness of a selected approach. Although not all school leaders expect school counselors to carry out their jobs using this transformed vision, the school counseling community has been advocating for this approach for many years. Their efforts are supported by data showing that effective school counseling programs have a positive effect on a range of academic outcomes, including increased math and reading proficiency, higher graduation rates, and better organizational and study skills such as time use, persistence, note taking, and test taking.[33] One of the many benefits of the evidence-based school counseling movement is greater clarity of counselor impact.

Collectively, the evolution of the school counseling profession illustrates how forces in education and beyond broadened counselors' responsibilities to bring about a profession responsible for three primary domains: academic, social emotional, and postsecondary. Given the interconnectedness of these domains and the reality that students' development in one domain is inextricably linked to development in another domain, the multidomain scope makes sense. However, as counselors' scope expanded, support for their new roles has not kept pace.

MOVING BEYOND THE CATEGORIES: INTRODUCING SUPPORT FOR THE ROLE

By expanding the scope of their functions beyond the original focus on vocational development, school counselors have enabled schools to respond to new societal demands and needs of students. However, as school counseling expectations grew and took shape during the mid to late 1900s, educators quickly realized that the profession needed additional structure and support for the ever-growing and diverse role. Three major forces contributed to the formalization of the multifaceted counseling role that continues today: the establishment of professional organizations, the development of comprehensive guidance and counseling models, and the formalization of preservice training.

Professional Organizations

The evolution of school counselors' role was supported by many professional organizations, especially those that helped integrate the distinct components of the role and gave the profession legitimacy. The largest and most comprehensive of these is the American School Counselor Association, which has led the profession throughout the better part of school counseling's history. Chartered as a division of what is today the American Counseling Association (ACA), ASCA's National Standards identify key content for school counseling programs; ensure all students have equitable access to counseling professionals; and outline the attitude, knowledge, and skills students should gain from participating in a comprehensive school counseling program. Nine specific standards were established in 1997 falling under three domains—academic, career, and personal/social development. These standards have been especially critical in drawing clear links between counseling and academic achievement.

Comprehensive and Developmental Models

During the 1970s and 1980s, an economic recession, combined with a decline in school enrollments, led to reductions in the number of school staff in communities around the country. In this context of cost cutting, many in education began to question the overall usefulness of school counselors, including the effectiveness of counseling practices. The profession responded with efforts to clarify its role, including the introduction of comprehensive and developmentally focused counseling programs that addressed the specific manner in which school counseling programs met the needs of all students across multiple domains.

Counselor educator Norman Gysbers is credited with establishing the basis for all subsequent counseling models through his original comprehensive guidance model. Gysbers first developed this model with funding from the US Office of Education to assist all fifty states plus the District of Columbia and Puerto Rico to develop "models or guides for implementing career guidance, counseling and placement programs in local schools."[34] From this project, a manual was developed in 1974 outlining the organizational structure of what would become the premier model for a comprehensive guidance program. This comprehensive guidance model, still widely used today, gives counselors a blueprint for organizing their program content, resources, program management, and accountability.

Drawing on their professional standards, as well as work by Gysbers and Henderson, ASCA ultimately developed the *ASCA National Model*, a framework adopted by many states and used by schools and districts for designing, implementing, and evaluating comprehensive K–12 counseling programs. The model consists of four quadrants (foundation, delivery system, management system, and accountability), each of which addresses a specific aspect of programming that is essential to help all students succeed academically.[35] Each model contributes to the content areas covered in training programs, through in-service and preservice opportunities, and guides the practices of school counselors in many schools today.

Today, many school counselors carry out comprehensive school counseling programs. In fact, at least thirty states have instituted these programs, which ASCA defines as "comprehensive in scope, preventative in design and developmental in nature."[36] Guided by the ASCA National Standards and the ASCA National Model, these programs have given school counselors structure and guidance to run their programs and, in some cases, professionalized the field of school counseling. The degree to which schools adopt and implement this model varies, and certainly, not all schools adhere to it; however, the ASCA National Model provides important guidance to counselors' practice and is the leading model in use.

Preservice Training

Formal training for school counselors gained momentum following the formal establishment of a professional organization (ASCA) in 1952 and funding through the National Defense Education Act (NDEA) in 1958, which provided funds to train school counselors at the university level and to develop "Counseling and Guidance Training Institutes" in 1959.[37] These formal training opportunities, originally limited to teachers, were further influenced by the birth of counseling theories, the standardized testing movement, and laws protecting children from abuse or neglect.[38] Because the impetus for graduate training coincided with the addition of personal and mental health training, graduate programs were developed to prepare for this counseling role, drawing often on counseling theorists and psychopathology. As such, many programs have leaned heavily on counseling and psychology courses into modern times, even as the role of counselors has expanded beyond this domain.

In the late 1990s, a nationally known educational policy group, the Education Trust, questioned whether this emphasis on counseling approaches in graduate education was serving students well.[39] Prior research by the Education Trust had found that although these graduate programs offered sufficient mental health and social emotional training, they inadequately prepared counselors to serve as academic advisors and advocates and, especially, to use data in their advocacy efforts and student support initiatives. The Education Trust argued that by ensuring training programs provide aspiring counselors with the proper skills and knowledge, these professionals can then effectively support the achievement and attainment of marginalized students within their schools and districts. The Education Trust, in partnership with the DeWitt Wallace-Reader's Digest Fund, launched the Transforming School Counseling Initiative in 1997 to reframe the role of the school counselor in the US education system, which included major changes to counselor education programs.[40]

Although the Transforming School Counseling Initiative brought about changes to counselor education, many educators continued to criticize counselor training programs for not preparing their students for the realities of the job. In a 2011 College Board report entitled *Counseling at a Crossroads*, the authors reported that only 16 percent of school counselors rated their graduate training as highly effective.[41] These criticisms were largely attributed to the fact that graduate programs were not following one unified set of guidelines or competencies.

Today, variation still exists in counselor education programs. Some graduate programs align their curriculum with standards set by state boards of education, whereas others follow both state guidelines and those set by the Council for Accreditation of Counseling and Related Educational Programs, a counseling accreditation program that established training standards for school counseling programs. Although graduate coursework varies by state and institution, most offer courses in clinical counseling topics and theories (individual, group, cross-cultural), psychological testing, legal and ethical issues, and career development. Calls for more attention to cultural competence, counselor leadership, data-driven practices, and college-readiness counseling have brought about changes to some graduate curricula. For example, at one time, counselor education programs neglected coursework related to college counseling completely, instead favoring a more traditional career development curriculum. In a study conducted by NACAC in 2004, the organization's researchers found that only twenty-three colleges offered college admissions counseling coursework at the graduate level, and only four of these colleges required the counselors to take these courses. Now, the tide seems to be turning on this, evident in a 2016 report published by the Council of National School Counseling and College Access Organizations, which found that among forty-two graduate-level counseling programs, the majority of programs *did* address college access and admission counseling competencies, although to varying extents.[42] This adjustment to graduate training reflects a willingness on the part of higher education to align coursework with counselors' updated roles in schools. These are baby steps; however, these changes lay the foundation for additional updates to how preservice counselors are trained.

MOVING FROM *SPUTNIK* TO TODAY: COUNSELORS' READINESS FOR CHANGE

While the school counseling profession has been evolving and expanding in scope and size, the federal government has played a limited supporting role. To date, the biggest federal contribution to school counseling followed the Soviet Union's launching of *Sputnik 1* in the late 1950s. The National Defense Act, which Congress passed in response to the satellite launch, stemmed from a perceived national security threat of "Soviet educational superiority."[43] The act aimed to make America more competitive by identifying academically talented students and preparing them for careers in strategic fields including math, science, engineering, and modern foreign language. It included millions of dollars for strengthening school counseling programs. In fact, a focus on counselor recruitment and training increased the size of the profession nearly threefold in the span of a decade. The legislation also funded training institutes designed to improve the qualifications and increase the number of counselors in secondary schools capable of working with "academically able students"—defined as pupils qualified for college-level studies.[44] With the federal money and attention to the profession, school counseling increased in consistency across the country. Counselor education programs were formed to adequately prepare professionals for this new and uniquely defined role.

Yet, since that time, the federal government has not made a targeted commitment to invest in the readiness or efficacy of school counseling. Certainly, the Education for All Handicapped Children Act of 1975, the Family Educational Rights and Privacy Act of 1974, the Americans with Disabilities Act of 1990, and the Individuals with Disabilities Education Act affirmed the role of counselors in supporting the achievement of all students, including those with disabilities. Likewise, the Carl D. Perkins Vocational Education Act of 1984 authorized funding to support career and technical education. However, these efforts did not specifically provide support for the professionalization of school counseling programs or the professionals who deliver counseling services. Rather, these policies provide direction, guidance, and sometimes funding for particular programming or policies to be implemented by school counselors. The absence of more systemic investments in school counseling since the National Defense Act in 1958 raises a question: What *would* it take for our nation, school districts, and schools to deeply invest in the profession once again?

Sixty plus years after the launching of *Sputnik*, our country is again at a critical juncture. Instead of a Russian satellite, the impetus is our own students calling out for change, in the form of better academic, social emotional, and postsecondary support. We have a student body whose needs are more complex than ever. Today, we expect school counselors to work across these three domains, attending to the complexities of supporting transgender youth who are bullied, helping first-generation college-bound students aspire to and plan for higher education, and identifying appropriate interventions for academically challenged students. However, if counselors are going to successfully meet these expectations, our nation's schools, districts, and departments of education will need to be a part of that change. Carol Dahir, a leader in school counseling, has said that the school counseling profession has been on a journey for many years.[45] Indeed, the counselors' role has been shaped, redefined, and expanded by many forces outside the profession during this journey, with little coherence, support, or unifying vision to meet these expectations.

Societal changes and shifts have brought increased expectations of schools, many of which have fallen to school counselors. This layering on of the role is grounded in counselors' unique position to support students across multiple domains. However, while counselors have tried to keep pace with these new demands, they have not been matched by a comprehensive vision or appropriate supports.

I believe counselors are ready for change and a unified vision that matches the expectations of everyone from policy makers to district leaders. Many reports published on the state of school counseling include the voices and perspectives of counselors and leaders in the profession who believe that they can and should do better. Even more telling was the enormous response to then First Lady Michelle Obama's Reach Higher initiative. At their own expense, hundreds of practicing school counselors and counseling leaders flocked to national and regional convenings to recommit to improving their college and career-readiness counseling. There was a readiness among this group to extend counseling work in research, practice, and policy. This public awareness is an opportunity not seen since the *Sputnik* moment in the 1950s, and one that has opened a crucial opportunity for the counseling profession.

In spite of this mounting excitement and interest, counselors can't make the change on their own. While the profession has grown significantly, the broader educational system has not taken the full step of examining and investing in the school counseling profession. To fully implement the progress we have made and all that school counselors have to offer, it is time to tackle the systemic barriers that undermine the work. Michelle Obama, who often referred to herself as the "school counselor in chief," had this to say about the current system:

> [W]hen the average student-to-counselor ratio in this country is 471 to 1—and in some places, there's only 1 counselor for every 1,000 students—let's just stop there for a moment as we think about the goals we want our kids to achieve and just think about what we're asking these men and women to do—when too many counselors just don't have what they need to do their jobs. When we look at all of that, what we know is that we still have a lot of work to do.[46]

With professionals who are ready for more and the public starting to understand the need for the work of counselors, we need new ideas. Using an old model to address current challenges won't work. Today's challenges depend on a new solution, and counselors are schools' largest untapped resource. As former First Lady Michelle Obama suggests, it's time to get to work.

2

✦

SCHOOL COUNSELING REENVISIONED

Using the Academic Home Approach

When I met Marianna, she was in the ninth grade, and she was bright, friendly, responsible, and eager to do well in school.[1] Shortly after meeting her, I encouraged her to participate in an early college awareness program I was running on Saturdays, and through this experience, I began to build a relationship with her. Over the next two years, I continued to support Marianna's academic engagement and her commitment to be the first in her family to attend college. Marianna loved writing and dreamed of going to college to become a writer.

During our conversations, Marianna shared that she had a strained relationship with her mom; she hinted that her mom used drugs and dated men that she and her sisters did not like. When I pursued these topics, Marianna insisted everything was fine, describing her experience as "typical stuff." But at the start of her junior year, Marianna told me that her mom's drug use had gotten worse and that one of the boyfriends had been abusive to her and her mother. This disclosure prompted me to file a report with the state child welfare agency, and ultimately, Marianna and her younger sister were placed in foster care. This was an extremely difficult time for Marianna. Her foster mother was cruel, and Marianna became increasingly less hopeful about her future.[2] Fortunately, one of Marianna's strengths was her ability to ask for help, and she sought me out often. I *knew that I could refer her to the school psychologist; however, Marianna made it very clear that she would not meet with anyone else. I believed that I could continue to let her know she was loved and that school was a safe place for her and to hold her to high expectations.*

Marianna continued to pursue her academic goals, but when she was sixteen, she came to me confused, angry, and deeply scared. She had requested her birth certificate for job applications and had learned something her mom had kept from her for many years: Marianna was undocumented. Her mother had brought her and her sister to the United States on vacation, and they had never returned to their home in the Dominican Republic. Mariana was devastated. She quickly surmised that this could impact her dream of going to college. What could she do? Had her chances of going to college disappeared?

I did all I could to support Marianna. Immediately, I began researching supports for undocumented students and their work and college options. I called social workers, immigration experts, and even lawyers. With Marianna, I discussed the difficulties of being in foster care and what she could do if she couldn't attend college. We spoke often of her academic classes, but I saw her become more and more disengaged from school. Eventually, our appointments turned into long discussions about hopelessness, and I worried about her mental health. I often suggested she see a mental health counselor to which she would reply, "I am. I am seeing YOU."

As her school counselor, I was, in fact, a mental health counselor to Marianna—and a school counselor, academic advisor, and case worker. Yet, I knew that even with the significant amount of time I was spending on her case, I was not able to fully address all of her needs, especially her mounting depression. Worse, all my time with Marianna meant less time for other students. As one person with a huge range of responsibilities and students, I couldn't provide every support Marianna needed. But what if I had been able to coordinate those supports, to be the glue that would connect all the pieces she needed? Most school counselors don't have the resources or opportunities to make that happen, but we could learn a lot from another profession that does: medicine.

Most people reading this likely have experience with primary health care, namely through your primary care physician, or PCP. This primary care model enables you to connect with a single person, your PCP, who can coordinate all your medical care and connect you to the right specialist at the right time. PCPs provide as much care as they can themselves, but when you need more intensive or specialized treatment—say, for a torn knee ligament or progressive heart disease—they refer you to an orthopedist or a cardiologist. This system is so commonplace that it may surprise you that it is relatively recent. Until fifty or sixty years ago, access to medical professionals was spotty and highly inequitable—much as it is today for student access to school counselors. After World War II, patients tended to seek care from disconnected specialists—in part because the specialist sector grew when physicians who had served in the military were provided funds to undertake specialist postgraduate training and in part because of the rise of a fee-for-service private insurance system.[3] This system led to highly inequitable health care within and across nations, and ultimately, the medical profession moved away from a model dominated by specialist physicians and toward a primary health model. That system has provided a number of benefits, especially continuity of care for patients' many diverse needs.

In this book, I propose that school counselors could work more efficiently, and students could be served more effectively, if school counselors act more like primary care physicians. In particular, we could benefit from an approach similar to one known as the "medical home." The Patient-Centered Medical Home Model (PC-MH)—more simply known as the medical home—is a holistic, team-based care delivery model that was designed to help overcome the challenges physicians faced in providing effective, high-quality primary care. Developed by the American Academy of Pediatrics in 1967, this model aims to ensure that all patients have access to a personal physician who is their first point of contact in the health system and who oversees the management of their care.

Patients are typically supported by a physician-led team composed of nurse practitioners, nurses, physician assistants, and other health professionals who work in tandem to deliver care at all stages of the life course (e.g., acute, chronic, behavioral, end-of-life care, and preventative services) and, when appropriate, coordinate patient care for services provided outside the PC-MH.[4] Perhaps not surprisingly, a wide body of evidence indicates the PC-MH model reduces health-care costs and hospitalization rates, while improving quality and patient experiences.[5] In fact, the medical home model is the fastest-growing primary care delivery system implemented in the United States.[6]

In the same way that primary care physicians offer people a medical home, school counselors are well positioned to offer students an "academic home." Today's students need professionals who can respond to the myriad issues they bring to school that get in the way of their learning. They depend on counselors to promote many types of skills and competencies that are conducive to their academic and personal health.

In this chapter, I describe how a clarified and strategic role for school counselors can be viewed much like the medical home model for physicians whereby counselors act as generalists, providing a consistent, trusted base of support while also referring students to specialized supports when necessary. Here, I present why aspects of school counseling are particularly suited to this analogy. Because our school system is not yet designed to fully implement and support such a model, this chapter explains how we can change that and provide the infrastructure and supports that can allow school counselors and, most importantly, their students to be more successful.

ENVISIONING AN ACADEMIC HOME FOR STUDENTS

What would an academic home in the school counseling office look like? What would it have looked like for Marianna? It might have looked something like the following: As a member of a functional student support team, I would have brought forth her case and identified at least two specialists who could have helped her with (1) immigration issues and (2) emerging mental health concerns. Through that team or other collaborative structures, I would be kept abreast of her progress so that I could incorporate that information into my ongoing, comprehensive support for Marianna. In addition, communication with specialists would signal to Marianna that a team of people was supporting her.

We can extrapolate a great deal from the medical home model to inform a similar academic home model for use by school counselors. The focus of the medical home on ensuring an equitable, accessible, and comprehensive delivery of services to a wide range of individuals mirrors the goal that school counselors set for their work with students. Yet, the value of drawing on the medical home model is in identifying the system that supports such a unified practice. Importantly, the academic home, similar to the primary health care model, embodies a set of ideas and qualities about how practitioners can work together to meet individual and community needs. The value to school counseling, then, is to identify those specific qualities and conditions that need to be met for an academic home to reach its desired goal of meeting students' academic, social emotional, and postsecondary needs. Although intended for a patient-physician relationship, the core tenets of the medical home are surprisingly relevant to school counselor–student relationships as well.

Ongoing, Trusting Relationships

The medical home model is driven by a patient-centered philosophy, in which patients are seen as equal partners with health-care professionals and in which their needs are the driver of care decisions.[7] In this way, physicians partner with patients to deliver care that addresses the health of the whole person. A version of this idea has been gaining traction in education through a focus on student-centered learning, or the process of shifting the focus of instruction from the teacher to the student. This is also evident in the growing body of research on teacher-student relationships for learning and creating a sense of connectedness in school. In the field of counseling, this concept has deep roots in psychology through the work of Carl Rogers, who advanced the idea of a person-centered approach to counseling. According to Rogers, a psychologist who is considered the pioneer of humanist psychology, individuals are primarily responsible for their own learning and behavior. The work of the counselor, then, is to set the conditions for each person to find fulfillment, happiness, and success. This work happens today through the way counselors structure their meetings with students, engage students in student voice and leadership projects, and even facilitate student-led parent-teacher conferences.

Certainly, trust is the cornerstone to all helping relationships. When school counselors are able to form trusting relationships with students, they are especially positioned to meet students' varying needs. Let me offer two illustrations of why this is the case. First, schools depend on school counselors to create spaces where students can disclose personal information in service to getting help. Whether that information is domestic violence as in the case of Marianna, bullying and harassment from another student, or fear about coming out to one's parents, school counselors place a high value on building trust. That trust, often built over several years, enables counselors to connect students to the right supports when necessary. Often, students' willingness to seek support from those specialists is influenced by the level of trust they have with their counselor.

Second, trusting relationships form the basis for the important transmission of social capital. Human capital theorists emphasize that social capital, or the tacit body of knowledge one acquires through relationships with others, is essential for first-generation college-bound students.[8] In essence, the presence of trust facilitates the transmission of information, expectations, and support about a process for which a student may have limited knowledge or experience. In my experience, this type of trust is what made my students, who were generally the first in their family to attend college, accept my high expectations and college knowledge. In short, the trusting relationships formed from ongoing care establish the basis for counselors to execute the range of responsibilities placed on them, from creating safe learning spaces to promoting career and future possibilities.

Care Coordination

Another core tenet of the medical home model is care coordination, which refers to how physicians coordinate patient care across the larger health system and connect individuals to specialized care. In the medical home, emphasis is placed on establishing clear lines of communication among patients, families, the medical home, and other providers. This model ensures individuals have a "home" where they are known by one person and where they trust that many people are working together to ensure their needs are being met. One benefit is continuity over time; having the same provider over multiple years offers patients the chance to build trust, share health history, and ensure their provider sees them in a holistic manner. School counselors can provide this same kind of continuous support. Unlike teachers who have different students every year, or even every semester, school counselors typically work with students for their entire experience at one school. Because counselor assignments are often made based on family name, this results in counselors working with students' siblings year after year, thus working with the same parents and caregivers.

In schools, coordination of care is more important today than ever and may be the most essential tenet to enact from the medical home model. Specialized supports are vital because it is unrealistic for counselors to develop expertise in the wide range of needs students bring to school. As a counselor, I can recall working with an emancipated minor to complete financial aid forms and lacking expertise in the laws surrounding that student's unique rights. I also worked closely with a student who suffered from extreme social anxiety, but I wasn't trained in the cognitive behavioral therapy she needed. In both cases, I depended heavily on specialists from the community. In the case of the emancipated minor, I collaborated with a nonprofit that had expertise in financial aid and affordability. In the case of the student struggling with social anxiety, I recall many conversations with her team of teachers to help them understand how her anxiety affected her schoolwork and ultimately referred her to an outside social service agency for therapy. Yet, all too often this type of referral is not managed in an ongoing manner. Unless I asked the student for an update, I rarely knew the outcome or progress of these cases, limiting my ability to ensure follow-through. Generally, these services were disconnected from schools, limiting opportunities for connection between outside services and in-school experiences. When counselors lead a network of providers, build relationships with them, and develop systems for communication, they are better able to capitalize on the expertise of different organizations and professionals.

Coordinating student support services is especially vital in light of the rise in community-based partners and specialists who work in and with schools. In many parts of the country, schools are surrounded by numerous community partners who specialize in a range of educational, social emotional, and postsecondary preparation areas. Yet typically, schools lack clear systems to manage and leverage these specialists. Many counselors in large urban centers describe not even knowing some of the agencies that are working in their buildings. Instead, schools tend to treat each additional support as an add-on with little integration.

Some models, including integrated support services, in which a constellation of people and programs work with students over time and share information, are promising, however. Some schools operate highly functional student support teams. These teams, which often include teachers, school staff and representatives from outside agencies, and school partners offering targeted support services, convene to discuss students presenting academic or behavioral concerns.

Finally, a break came for Marianna. In the spring of her junior year, I learned about an organization called Massachusetts Immigrant and Refugee Association (MIRA), which supported immigrant populations and specifically had a program for undocumented students. In addition to signing up Marianna for a program with MIRA, I developed a relationship with one of the staff members. We talked often regarding information about Marianna and shared concerns about her future. It was during one of those late afternoon phone calls when a sliver of hope appeared.

Marianna had not shared with the MIRA staff member that she was living in foster care. Without that information and related information that Marianna's foster mom restricted her time in out-of-school activities, the staff member had grown frustrated by Marianna's absence at several events at which she was expected. After securing permission from Marianna, I shared this information with the staff member in the hopes that it would ensure Marianna could stay in the program. As it turns out, sharing that information did a lot more than keep her in the program.

That day on the phone, I learned that when children are in the custody of the state, as is the case when they are in foster care, the state can petition for their citizenship. That meant it was possible for Marianna and her sister to begin the process of securing their documentation as legal US residents. Together with MIRA, we worked with a social worker at the state child welfare organization who understood this provision and supported pursuing it. Over the course of the next year, I spent a lot of time communicating by phone and in person with her social worker, state attorney, and others.

In the fall of her senior year, Marianna and her sister were granted legal residency as wards of the state. Even better, they were later reunited with their mother and returned to their home. In her senior year, Marianna was admitted to college to study nursing, a career she continues to love today.

Fundamentally, students' chances for success increase when adults work together to coordinate and collaborate their programming. This was true in my case with Marianna, as it was with many other students with whom I worked. Being able to collaborate with community partners, advocates, lawyers, social service agencies, and afterschool programs made my job easier and created seamless experiences for students. During that experience, I thought nothing of the time and energy I spent searching for an organization to support Marianna, talking with MIRA staff and attorneys, and translating across sectors to work together toward the same goal. Looking back, however, I realize my deep involvement also meant less time for other students.

From afterschool program coordinators and mental health counselors to tutors and job placement supervisors, students benefit from a team of people who share responsibility for their success. Nonetheless, the system that enables collaboration needs to be stronger and more efficient. Counselors should be positioned to implement clear memoranda of agreement between partners, manage data systems that track students' affiliation with various programs, and lead meetings that bring together a team that works in academic, social emotional, and postsecondary domains. Likewise, the many partners, collaborators, and specialists that work with students need to understand their role in helping the counselor coordinate this care. This role might include attending team meetings, using technology, or managing communication and tracking systems. Without clear systems for collaboration such as teams or formalized partnerships, these efforts can take up a lot of time, or worse, they don't happen at all. An academic home approach can help bring these systems and practices into the mainstream.

Comprehensive Care

Comprehensive care, another fundamental aspect of the medical home, refers to how the model meets an individual's holistic physical and mental health needs through offering preventative services as well as targeted interventions and support. To accomplish this, medical homes are composed of a primary care physician who offers preventative care and screening and a team of a health professionals who together deliver comprehensive care through specialized practices. Enacting an academic home vision suggests that school counselors deliver prevention programming to all students on their caseload in addition to responsive services.

Sometimes referred to as universal programming or Tier 1 supports, these practices promote students' development through classroom lessons, individualized student plans, and schoolwide events.

Applying the comprehensive care quality to school counseling also means clarifying that counselors' roles must extend across the three domains of academic, social emotional, and postsecondary development, which are interconnected, as illustrated in the case of my former student, Marianna. Counselors often experience what researchers refer to as cascade theory, a concept that describes how development in one part of a person's life influences development in another aspect. Student development across many facets—biological, cognitive, social, emotional— is interconnected, and thus, when counselors support students in one aspect of their lives, this support can also have an influence on other aspects. For example, after I connected a reserved, insecure rising tenth grader to a summer leadership program, she returned in the fall with a positive self-concept and belief in herself, which influenced her academic performance the following year.

Schools have begun to recognize the value of these theories, and some schools are now designed around the idea of being hubs of student support.[9] A growing number of educational settings, such as community schools and the Harlem Children's Zone, provide wraparound services to students and families in a given geographical area. The idea behind these models is that when kids have their primary needs met, they are set up to learn and thrive in school. School counselors can be better utilized in these models, especially because they interact with students across the school over multiple years and interact with them across the three domains.

Accessibility

One of the primary benefits of the medical home model is increased access to a single health professional who has background knowledge and history of a patient and can provide access to specialized supports. Accordingly, accessibility is characterized in the medical home as providing patients with greater access to health services through shorter waiting times, expanded hours, and better communication between patients and physicians.[10] Whereas the specifics of how this model is implemented might differ in schools, accessibility is improved in the academic home approach when students are able to access a school counselor who knows them and can connect them to specialized support services essential to their success in school and beyond.

Increasing students' access to a school counselor happens when counselors have more time for their full caseload because they share responsibility for student development with many partners. For instance, when counselors attempt to provide targeted, time-intensive supports to some students, it leaves little time to meet all students on their caseload or provide broad, preventative programming. Also, whereas counselors aim to be highly accessible and responsive to the majority of their students' needs, the conditions in schools and expectations of partners have undermined this goal. For example, counselors' accessibility is limited when they are assigned testing and administrative duties that fill time otherwise spent with students. Yet, making counselors the center of academic supports can increase their visibility and accessibility.

Increasing accessibility also refers to how a coordinated approach can create equal access to all the specialists in the network. In this book, I have argued that the current state of community partner involvement can lead to fragmentation and unequal access to services. This fragmentation happens when the pathways to connect with school-based partners are informal and not managed to ensure equity. For example, many enrichment programs depend on student self-selection for participation. With a centralized coordinating structure, which would be fundamental in an academic home approach, school counselors could use data to ensure that all students have access to the additional supports they need to thrive.

Quality Monitoring

The final tenet of the medical home model is a commitment to quality improvement to improve patient experiences and satisfaction. Applying this idea to school counseling can highlight the important function of school counselors using data for continuous improvement and serving as leaders and advocates for change. School counselors are increasingly expected to utilize practices that are empirically grounded and scientifically based.[11] Data- and standards-driven decision-making is a core element of the ASCA National Model.[12] Yet, whereas many school counselors report being interested in using data to drive programming and communicate the influence of their work, they also report lacking confidence in their research and evaluation competencies.[13] Using the medical home model focus on quality monitoring and improvement can help counseling emphasize data-driven practice and therefore make available the training and systems to support it. Just as important, quality evaluation practices can create an accountability system for counselors.

CONCEIVING OF THE ACADEMIC HOME AS AN APPROACH, NOT A PRESCRIPTIVE MODEL

Before outlining the steps and supports for enacting the academic home concept in school counseling, I want to explain why this way of thinking about school counseling is not meant to be a prescriptive definition or model. The evolution of school counseling reflects a profession that has taken on increased responsibilities in response to societal concerns devoid of a shared vision or set of structures to meet those expectations. The idea of an academic home provides a framework for those outside the school counseling community to understand the counselor's role and gives those within it language to communicate their needs to others. Instead of a model with strict guidelines about how things should operate, I believe students would benefit from all educators embracing an updated way of thinking about counselors and their work in schools.

This updated vision is especially applicable in a professional context in which there is great variation among counselors' roles and work experiences across geographic area or grade level. For example, I can imagine that counselors working in rural areas might question the feasibility of building teams of community partners given limited resources and wide geographic coverage. However, if we consider a few characteristics common in rural schools, the academic home still creates a guiding vision for their work. Even though in some rural areas one counselor is responsible for the whole school, sometimes even the entire district, that counselor can still provide continuity of care for students across K–12 to deeply connect with students. In addition, rural schools often act as hubs of support for the community when other resources are scarce. Dee Hann-Morrison, who writes extensively about rural school counselors, describes rural communities' reliance on schools as a "type of kinship of care" that reflects the ways in which schools support community and individual community members' needs.[14] Accordingly, counselors see this bridging as part of their role. Thus, rural school counselors are likely providing comprehensive supports, a key feature of an academic home. In a resource-scarce environment, this support can include partnering with teachers in their buildings through advisories and other forms of distributive counseling.

Using an approach that puts counselors in a leadership role to provide the first line of support to students, while drawing on the contributions of partners, is vital given the scope of counselors' role. Due to the increased demands placed on schools, counselors are currently expected to provide both depth and breadth of services with a relatively large caseload. In other words, they are asked to perform an impossible feat. It is hard to imagine how counselors in Arizona, where caseloads exceed nine hundred students, would provide even light-touch supports to all their students.[15] Certainly, counselors can provide an individual student multiple types of support over the course of that individual's academic career; however, that is a difficult feat for a single counselor to accomplish with four hundred students, the current national average.[16] One solution has been to introduce additional specialists to take on various aspects of counselors' duties. This approach has reduced the burden on counselors; however, it has the potential to create fragmentation, promote an inequity of services, and undermine a coordinated support network. Another strategy has been to limit the domains in which counselors' work, relieving them of their mental health responsibilities or the college counseling function. However, given the interconnected nature of development, such an approach is misguided and risks losing the benefit of trusting relationships in one domain that opens the door for students to seek help in other domains, as was the case for Marianna. An academic home approach keeps school counselors in the nexus of students' complete schooling experience.

The recognition of the key role of teachers, school leaders, community partners, philanthropists, and policy makers is a hallmark of the academic home concept. Acknowledging this ecology surrounding students is crucial to counselors' effectiveness, and yet, little attention has been given to how changes in their practices can positively influence counselors' work with students. By articulating the ways in which schools, districts, policy makers, and philanthropists need to function together to support students, the academic home can quicken the pace of improved student outcomes. These ecological systems include the district-level supports and structures, school-level organizational features and practices, professional development and training, and state and federal policies that create the conditions for school counselors to effectively work with higher than recommended caseloads, while also providing comprehensive supports. In this way, an academic home complements other models used in the field by acknowledging those who work with and in support of students and counselors.

Along the same lines, with a growing number of specialists engaged in academic, social emotional, and postsecondary domains, this updated vision will also go a long way in ensuring that role responsibilities are clear. From school-based staff such as teachers, school nurses, and speech therapists to outside partners such as college access advisors, mental health providers, and academic tutoring programs, school counselors have many partners with whom they can coordinate. With clarity of role and a leader guiding these collective efforts, as is suggested by an academic home vision, role confusion, duplication of efforts, or missed opportunities for collaboration are less likely to occur.

For counselors who may already be operating in this way, this orientation can help them articulate their role to school and district leaders and community partners so they improve their understanding of what counselors do and how to collaborate with them in service to students. Moreover, this way of envisioning the field can complement and work with existing models and standards. For example, this approach aligns well with the ASCA National Model that guides school counselors' work across academic, social emotional, and postsecondary domains and emphasizes counselors' role as leaders, advocates, and data-informed professionals.

Although the medical home model offers an analogy that can inform a vision for school counseling, this concept is not completely transferable. An important distinction between the comprehensive care aspect of the medical home model and current school counseling is the entry point. Primary care providers are patients' first point of contact in the health system. As such, these providers are highly accessible and capable of addressing the majority of patients' personal health needs. Primary care physicians also refer patients to specialists, hospitals, treatment centers, and community organizations that can effectively ameliorate issues that fall outside the purview of primary care practices.[17] Unlike primary care physicians, counselors are not always students' first or only point of entry in a network of student supports and programming. In some cases, students are referred to nonprofit or social service programs through other means such as churches or community centers. Most schools lack a system to ensure their community partners keep them informed about students' progress. In a perfectly organized world, counselors would serve as the only point of entry, thereby maintaining data and expectations for coordination and communication. Unfortunately, that is unlikely to change. Instead, the challenge for educators is to create systems that promote equitable access to partner programs and articulate clear feedback loops regardless of the referral source.

This distinction aside, the academic home concept provides a way of conceiving of school counseling that yields clear recommendations for school and district leaders, as well as other partners in student success.

BUILDING THE FOUNDATION FOR AN ACADEMIC HOME APPROACH

The field of school counseling is ripe for a paradigm shift to address the myriad constraints currently placed on the profession and role. Borrowing the concept of an academic home from the medical field, we can see how counselors are uniquely positioned to provide students an academic home by delivering comprehensive services, employing a student-centered approach to counseling, offering the continuity of care during their school years, and promoting accessibility and quality of services.

Conceiving of school counselors operating in this manner, similar to a primary care health provider, has the potential to improve students' access to and experiences with school-based supports at a time when such supports are sorely needed. However, like the medical home model, the promise of this approach depends heavily on the systems in which counselors work. That is, such a paradigm shift calls for changes among school and district leaders, community partners, policy makers, and even funders. What exactly are those changes, and what will it take to support an academic home and, more specifically, counselors' ability to offer an academic home? What structures need to be in place at the school and district levels? What is needed from funders and policy makers to ensure that counselors are trained adequately for such a role? In the next few chapters, I describe what changes need to happen in schools, districts, training programs, and even policy and philanthropic contexts in order for counselors to create an academic home for students. In particular, I highlight examples of the field where school counselors and others are using innovative strategies that offer lessons learned for those who want to try this approach.

3

❖

THE CREATION OF AN ACADEMIC
HOME NETWORK

Connecting Teachers, Community Organizations,
and Students

At Mount Baker High School, a team of school counselors, teachers, and a faculty member from Western Washington University led a major transformation of the school counseling program. Overwhelmed by the mental health needs of a few students and unable to address the needs of all, the two school counselors at this diverse rural high school decided to build a foundation for change to better meet the mental health concerns of their students. They knew the demands of proctoring standardized tests and the lack of a clear accountability system for counselors were getting in the way of meeting their students' growing needs, and yet they knew that the only way to address the gaps in services was to overhaul their program.

In 2004, when the teachers at Mount Baker were engaged in a data improvement process as a part of a district and state mandate, the school counseling department seized the opportunity to conduct an audit of their school counseling program. Two important findings gave them pause and inspired them to make a change. First, the counselors learned that students were not satisfied with the existing postsecondary planning they were receiving. Second, and perhaps most notably, they realized that the current emphasis on academic and postsecondary planning left them no time to implement social emotional counseling or programming, something both counselors knew was critical to students' academic success. The audit was just the nudge they needed to take action.

Over the course of the next six years, the counselors embarked on a process of change that included bringing new collaborations to the school to widen access to mental health services, distributing aspects of school counseling to teachers, and engaging students in leadership roles. Toby Marston, one of the school counselors at Mount Baker, described the process as "coalition building." For example, knowing that teachers were already informally involved in students' future planning through general relationship building, letters of recommendation, and unofficial advising, the counselors built out a robust advisory program that intentionally brought the teachers into the counselors' network of postsecondary supports. To maximize the potential of new community-based partners, the counselors also advocated for an improved data system, implemented group counseling sessions, and integrated data-driven practices to their programming.

Today, Marston and his colleagues play a different role in supporting all students in their school. Their network has grown, and they have additional professionals on staff, thanks to data showing the impact of mental health counselors.[1] With time, data, and a lot of effort, the counseling program at Mount Baker High School has been completely transformed.

The transformation at Mount Baker High School represents what is possible when school counselors envision their role as creating an academic home and are given the opportunity to make structural change. In this example, the focus was more about *how* the school counselors refocused their efforts than on *what* they were doing. The addition of new mental health supports from community programs was critical; however, an important element of this change process included how the counselors influenced multiple partners to support their goals. By tapping into the unique roles that teachers, parents, community partners, and even students themselves play, the school counselors created a coordinated and comprehensive counseling program that increased their accessibility and ensured they were using data to assess their effectiveness. As a result, they changed not only how they did their jobs but also how they thought about their role as system leaders and service providers.

Expecting school counselors to assume a leadership role does not mean that counselors are no longer working with students. In fact, quite the contrary. This example of an academic home in action illustrates how counselors can partner with students and remain accessible to them, while activating and deeply engaging with a strong network of specialized supports provided by teachers, community partners, and students.

Building the network of partners and developing the systems to support and coordinate them are central to this process. For the process to work, counselors can and should be central to identifying which partners are needed, brokering relationships with them, providing them clear expectations about what it means to work within the school community, and managing their services. When counselors are not involved in this process, as is sometimes the case, they report feeling that the presence of many partners undermines their own roles and removes them from the work they aspired to do when they entered the profession.

For an academic home approach to be successful, schools must be willing to differentiate the roles of counselors and their partners. One framework that illustrates such differentiation is the Multi-Tiered Systems of Support (MTSS) framework, in which schools provide services on a continuum from universal supports for all students (Tier 1) to targeted and intensive supports for students with higher levels of need (Tier 3). *Tier 1*, when applied to a counselors' role, includes supports designed to meet the needs of approximately 80 to 85 percent of students in a school, such as group seminar sessions and developmental school counseling curriculum delivery.[2] *Tier 2* includes individualized or targeted group interventions for the 10 to 15 percent of students whose academic, social emotional, or postsecondary needs are not fully served by Tier 1 supports.[3] These efforts include small-group counseling sessions for first-generation college-goers and "check-in/check-out," a widely implemented individualized intervention for students who struggle with behavior. In this intervention program, students check in each morning with a school adult and receive a blank report card that defines their behavior expectations and then check out with an adult in the afternoon to review the feedback teachers provided on the report card throughout the day.[4] *Tier 3* is geared toward the 3 to 5 percent of high-risk students who do not respond to either Tier 1 or Tier 2 interventions and thus require more intensive, individualized supports. These supports include one-on-one counseling or referrals to community agencies that can provide more intensive, long-term counseling and mental health services.[5]

School counselors are uniquely positioned to carry out Tier 1 and some Tier 2 supports across all three domains and to make referrals for Tier 3 supports provided by specialized providers. An MTSS approach—or what counselor educator Trish Hatch calls Multi-Tiered, Multi-Domain Systems of Supports (MTMDSS)—can help educators shift from trying to provide all services to coordinating the three tiers, providing some Tier 1 and 2 supports, while delegating and coordinating some Tier 2 and 3 services to teachers and community partners.[6] It was exactly this approach that was highly effective for Toby Marston and his colleagues at Mount Baker High School as they redesigned the school counseling work at their school.

As the historical evolution of the role has dictated, counselors are expected to provide both breadth and depth of services. Of course, they can't do it all. Fortunately, they don't have to. In this chapter, I describe how school counselors can create and lead networks that constitute an academic home and, importantly, how they can set in place systems to ensure that the network functions effectively. By employing the unique assets of teachers, community programs, and even students, counselors can ensure that all students have access to some type of support. As experts in the medical home model have found, the way the parts of the network interact is as important as the people and services within them.

School counselors and their partners can construct effective networks by using communication, teams, and partnership tools to build and manage a healthy system that works in service to all students.

DEFINING WHO'S IN

The first step to developing an academic home system for supporting students is to define the stakeholders and key partners who work with counselors to support student success.

Teachers

Teachers and school counselors have long partnered with one another to support students' success in school. From consulting with teachers about a struggling student to collaborating on a curriculum to promote study skills, counselors and teachers are key partners. In addition to the consultancy role that counselors play as a means of supporting teachers, counselors can also enlist teachers to deliver core elements of a counseling program. Many elementary school teachers already do this when they deliver social emotional lessons or career exploration activities. However, school counselors can leverage teachers' unique role and relationship with students in many more ways to ensure they have access to preventative and promotive lessons.

One way that school counselors can activate the unique contributions of teachers is through distributive counseling. Much like distributive leadership, in which shared, collective practices for decision-making and support build the capacity for change, distributive counseling is a process in which counselors empower and support others to engage in counseling-like work.[7] This strategy is particularly helpful for elementary school counselors, who are often responsible for an entire school, because it helps them reach more students while creating a supporting and caring school community. Because teachers are uniquely positioned in classrooms and develop strong relationships with students, they are

71

especially valuable partners in an academic home. For example, teachers can conduct screenings for students who may need additional support, deliver lessons that expose students to career possibilities, or even integrate developmental concepts into their curriculum and pedagogy.

Another way that school counselors can distribute their counseling work is by making sure that teachers and administrators understand how to help a diverse group of students. Accordingly, school counselors can research and disseminate information about populations heavily concentrated in their schools. For example, supporting students who are in foster care or have family members in the military requires some specific knowledge and expertise about these students. Here, a school counselor might notify a teacher that a student has a family member who has been deployed and encourage the teacher to ask questions about the deployed parent and the family, a practice that signals to students a genuine care and interest in their circumstances. Likewise, it might be important for counselors to educate teachers about the specific challenges faced by youth who live in foster care, may have attended multiple schools, and may struggle with an unstable living situation.

Danielle Duarte, a former elementary school counselor from California, believes that providing consultation to teachers is a great way to reach a wide group of students. An example of how Duarte approaches her work with teachers was evident when, following tragic wild fires in San Diego County, she created a guide for teachers and other school staff for talking with children. The opening of the guide provided important context:

> Teachers, please use this outline to have a conversation with your classroom about the recent North County fires that impacted many of our students and their families. This conversation is important because children need an opportunity to discuss their experiences in a safe, accepting environment. The classroom discussion also gives you a chance to clarify any misconceptions and discuss ways to help your students feel safe. Please adapt the information within the outline accordingly based on the developmental level of your students.

By suggesting to her teachers that kids need a safe space and giving them question prompts, Duarte is drawing on key partners to provide a service to her entire school. At the same time, Duarte also suggests to her teachers that they watch out for warning signs indicating that students might be struggling and provides recommendations for how to refer them to her and her colleagues if they are. In this way, she has set up a system for screenings and referrals.

We don't expect teachers to be trained in understanding the social and emotional impact of trauma or special needs of certain populations. However, this is where the academic home concept works best. School counselors can draw on the expertise of the network of partners in their community to bridge these knowledge gaps and ensure that the whole team is working together to support the individual students or groups of students.

Advisories are another type of distributive counseling that school counselors use to engage teachers in supporting students. The National Middle School Association defines an advisory as "an arrangement whereby one adult and a small group of students have an opportunity to interact on a scheduled basis in order to provide a caring environment for academic guidance and support, everyday administrative details, recognition, and activities to promote citizenship."[8] Sometimes called advocacy and teacher-based guidance programs, advisories are programs implemented at the middle and high school level.[9] They are premised on the idea that students benefit from having at least one trusted adult at school who can serve as their advocate; through helping students navigate their tumultuous middle and high school years, advisors promote the academic and social emotional development of their adolescent students.[10] Advisory programs help students adjust to school, build school culture, and foster a sense of belonging; they also support students' social emotional development and transition to postsecondary education.[11]

Although some schools have a loosely organized curriculum or even no formal advisory curriculum at all, others have implemented highly structured advisory programming developed by school personnel, districts, and nonprofit organizations like the College Board. Activities may include projects, written reflection, group discussions, interactive games, and community-building exercises that address topics such as goal setting, school citizenship, study skills, and postsecondary planning.[12] In many schools, counselors develop curriculum for teachers and provide consultation to them as they implement it. Although schools implement advisories in various ways, an advisory class often operates as a homeroom period.[13] Because the primary goal of advisories is to create relationships between students and staff, most are small, consisting of ten to twenty students. Whereas some schools schedule a fifteen- to thirty-minute advisory period daily, others reserve thirty to forty-five minutes for advisory a few times a week.[14]

Which school professionals are designated as advisors varies greatly. Teachers, administrators, librarians, coaches, aides, and even custodians and secretaries can serve as advisors. Although school counselors lead advisories in some places, in many places they do not. Instead, as Rachel Poliner and Carol Miller Lieber, researchers from Engaging Schools, note, "[I]n those schools, counselors can make themselves available to advisor groups for career and college discussions, or if needed, to help deal with the illness of a classmate, a horrible event in the world, or even a group dynamics problem within the group."[15]

I have visited some advisory programs that depend on school counselors to take a leadership or coordinating role within the program. They oversee the pairing of students with faculty or staff mentors, design the advisory curriculum, and offer training to advisors on topics as varied as effectively serving as an academic coach and interacting with parents and guardians.[16] This was the case for the counselors at Mount Baker High School.

When Toby Marston and his counselor colleague set out to transform their school counseling program to expand their reach to include mental health supports, they knew that implementing a teacher-run advisory program was crucial. They also knew that it would not be easy. Initially, Marston and his cocounselor spent a lot of time crafting lessons, which meant sacrificing time away from students. However, Marston felt this effort was a worthy investment of his time and set out to do whatever he could to set up teachers for a positive experience. Eventually, as the advisory program gained traction, the development of lessons became a shared responsibility with teachers.

Ultimately, an increase in family engagement convinced the teachers that the advisories were worthwhile. Historically, attendance at parent nights or parent-teacher meetings was not high. However, when the advisory teachers implemented student-run parent conferences, 90 percent of families attended. According to Marston, after that "it was hard to argue with the approach." To expand interest among other staff, he focused on the teachers who were successfully engaged and implementing the advisory: "Every time I talked with teachers about advisory, I would reference the teachers who implemented with fidelity. I highlighted where it was working." Now, with advisories well underway, Marston relies on a dedicated committee of teachers to write and adapt lessons, which has contributed to a culture of shared responsibility for advisories.

By distributing aspects of college and career planning to teachers, Marston admits that he is less familiar with and sees fewer of the high-achieving students. Yet, he describes this cost as worthwhile because they require less of him. Importantly, this shift has also freed up the counseling department to do other things that support their school counseling program, such as build new partnerships. Just as important, delivering postsecondary information through advisories gives the counselors the confidence that all students receive postsecondary planning information and the school feels they are better positioned to provide specialized supports.

Teachers are critical members of an academic home for many reasons. Typically, they are already engaged in some form of distributive counseling, building relationships and offering support to struggling students. When counselors formalize this role and provide the right structures and supports, students stand to benefit.

Community Partners

The expectation that counselors have to provide all student services themselves, so prevalent in schools today, makes it nearly impossible for counselors to do their work effectively. Using the academic home framework allows counselors to focus their efforts on providing universal supports and facilitating the service delivery of other, more targeted ones. For example, instead of conducting individual counseling with students who present symptoms of depression, counselors can utilize one of many depression screening tools to pinpoint students' specific needs and then connect students to community-based mental health services as needed. Similarly, instead of taking full responsibility for the many mechanical aspects of helping all students apply to college, counselors can figure out where their own time is best spent and refer students to community partners for specific components. For example, a counselor might choose to spend time helping a student determine future goals and then set up a time for that student to meet with a nonprofit partner that assists students in completing the complicated Free Application for Federal Student Aid (FAFSA). Or, a counselor might employ career exploration activities with ninth-grade students so as to set them up to participate in a career and technical education program sponsored by the state.

Many schools rely on contributions from university and community partners. College access programs, social service agencies, and community youth programs provide specialized supports that enhance school programming. As the history of school counseling revealed, an increase in student needs prompted schools to supplement school counseling programs through partnerships with other professionals. For example, in many schools, mental health counseling is managed and delivered by an outside party. Likewise, many schools have outsourced college planning supports to private college counselors and nonprofit programs.

These organizations play a powerful role in creating the network of supports critical to the success of an academic home framework. With unique specializations, community-based, federal and state-supported, and nonprofit organizations provide supports that often rely on specific knowledge outside the scope of a counselor's role or capacity.

In the postsecondary development domain, school counselors' work is supported by a range of organizations that share a vision and purpose with schools and school counselors. It is estimated that 1,650 college access or educational outreach programs exist in the United States.[17] This growing field is supported by the National College Access Network, a nonprofit organization that seeks to build the capacity of the college access community by sharing best practices; offering professional development; fostering collaboration across state, federal, and community programs; and advocating on issues related to college access. According to this organization, the college access field is made up of an array of community-based nonprofits, national nonprofits, local scholarship providers, state agencies, federally funded programs, K–12 schools, colleges, universities, and youth developmental programs. The majority of programs target high school students specifically and offer a range of services including academic support and college planning to strengthen students' college-going aspirations as well as academic preparation for postsecondary education. As a group, these organizations are ideal partners to integrate into an academic home model. However, successfully establishing that home depends on counselors' leadership in engaging and aligning the many parts of the network.

Many schools choose to actively partner with social service agencies and arrange for organizations to provide specific mental and physical health supports to their students. Results from the 2016 School Health Policies and Practices Study conducted by the US Centers for Disease Control and Prevention found that 49 percent of school districts offer mental health and social services to students through arrangements with outside organizations.[18] Approximately 36 percent of districts partner with local mental health or social service agencies, 32 percent with a local health department, and 20 percent with a community health clinic or health center.[19] The most common services offered included counseling, crisis intervention, assistance with accessing benefits for students with disabilities, identification of emotional or behavioral disorders, and administration of afterschool programs for students.[20]

When school counselors build a network of supports inside and outside of schools, they are better able to deliver preventative and developmental supports across all three domains of their work. For some school counselors, building a network with outside providers can be daunting, especially in a district that does not employ its own mental health counselors. Toby Marston, the rural school counselor introduced earlier, learned this very quickly.

The school counselors at Mount Baker High School knew they had mental health needs that were going unaddressed, thanks to a survey they conducted that showed students were struggling with anxiety, depression, and homelessness, among other emotional challenges. Yet, their location in northwest Washington state put them at a disadvantage in finding community partners. Although the rural school is located only fifteen miles from a small city, they felt they might as well be one hundred miles away given the dearth of outside agencies working with the school. As a result, Marston knew he had to convince new partners that this rural district was worth connecting with them. The counselors began by cold calling any public agency conducting counseling with kids. Although the initial response was slow, a few agencies responded favorably, and eventually, the school received seed money from a county-level mental health fund, which helped fund a half-time position.

Lack of familiarity with these new outside counselors and preexisting attendance issues meant that some kids needed help following up on appointments. Yet, Marston and his colleagues were determined to make sure the kids kept their appointments. On many occasions, upon learning that students had missed an appointment, Marston and his cocounselor would stop what they were doing and find kids who didn't show up. Eventually, the mental health counselors began to report better attendance rates at counseling sessions, which Marston partially attributes to the fact that he and his colleagues played a part in the handoff. "We would say to them, 'Hey, we think this would be good for you and here's why. Want to try meeting with them on your own, or with me there? Remember, if you don't want to meet them, just tell me."'

Marston and his cocounselor play a critical role in forming relationships with students, screening them for specialized needs, and then creating a bridge to additional supports. However, the work does not end there. The counselors made it clear to their partners that they want to stay in the loop, while respecting confidential information. This type of expectation has led to a collaborative partnership with community partners and a plan for communication.

For Marston, who is providing an academic home to students, getting students specialized services means finding time to deliver universal supports to more students. As a result, students get the diverse range of supports they need, and more students are served.

Building a network to support an academic home also provides a way to complement the skill set and capacity of school counselors. For instance, school counselors are often trained similarly to mental health counselors, receiving graduate coursework in counseling skills, psychopathology, and developmental interventions. However, school counselors cannot possibly be expert in everything. In Marston's case, this training enabled him to identify what supports were needed by what students and in what areas they needed additional support.

This practice of identifying students in need of specialized supports is growing in popularity as universal screening tools have become available. When counselors use screening tools for mental health concerns or other identified needs, they can identify students who are most in need of services and connect them to a network partner. For example, many school counselors implement depression or suicide screening tools with their students and use the results to identify students who might benefit from a group counseling program, further evaluation from a psychologist, or a referral to an outside therapist. However, successfully implementing these screening tools hinges on counselors having the time and space to do so. Teachers can be important partners in widescale implementation of screening tools and assessments.

Community partners can also support students by providing services that build schools' capacity to address specific issues. For example, Boston Children's Hospital Neighborhood Partnership provides professional development, consultation, and capacity building to school educators and leaders to promote students' social emotional and behavioral health. By offering professional development and ongoing capacity building, the partnership organization hopes that schools will be better able to address these issues themselves. Through a formal partnership, a school can receive up to 120 hours of consultation to support the creation of action plans to build sustainable systems within the school building.[21]

Fostering an academic home that effectively utilizes the unique contributions of many partners depends on a strong collaborative system. Sometimes, despite the best of intentions, these supplemental services lead to fragmentation and further dilute counselors' professional roles because the relationship between these programs and school counselors has not been well articulated. To avoid confusion or exacerbate inequities, school counselors and their partners need to communicate and articulate their roles and relationship between their work.

Students as Partners

One often overlooked resource that is essential to an academic home's network is students. Students can be an incredible support for their peers, and developmentally, this is an expected part of becoming an adolescent. Students can provide many different types of resources and opportunities for one another, including peer education and mentoring, especially "near-peer" mentor programs that capitalize on the closeness in age between students to promote effective transfer of information and support.

Community and nonprofit organizations are especially well suited to promote youth-led programming in schools and community settings. According to Janice Bloom, the codirector of College Access: Research and Action (CARA), a nonprofit program in New York City committed to supporting first-generation and low-income college-bound students' access to postsecondary opportunities and credentials, "youth can reach other youth in a way that adults can't."[22] CARA is known for incorporating youth/peer leadership into college access work in schools and higher education. In one of its primary programs, Right to College, CARA trains high school students to lead workshops and work individually with peers. This program has the dual goal of building leadership among students and building the capacity of schools to promote college-going cultures.[23] Importantly, this nonprofit has found that youth-led models work best when youth leaders receive clearly articulated roles, have time structured into their day to deliver the supports they were trained to provide, receive compensation in the form of credit or financial payment, and complete a robust training program.[24]

At CARA's Youth Leadership for College Access Summer Institute, young people from across New York City learned the knowledge and skills needed to work within their schools to help their peers through the postsecondary planning process. At this four-week intensive training institute, youth prepare for their role as peer leaders. The institute combines support for students' personal postsecondary planning process with training in college counseling content knowledge and skills. Specifically, they receive content-specific college knowledge while also developing important professional skills, such as communication with adults, communication with peers, advocacy, organization, self-reflection, public speaking, and perseverance. Not surprisingly, the youth complete the institute with a broadened understanding of the college planning process, a range of new skills to pass on to their classmates, and their own well-developed college application plans and materials.

When these trained seniors return to high school in the fall, they return as peer leaders, ready to help their classmates apply to and get through the college application process. These young people spend approximately eight to ten hours a week in a Student Success Center, which is staffed by a community-based college counselor and are paid for their time. However, their work is not limited to the centers. Reminders posted in the bathroom, help with applications over lunch, and encouraging nudges in the hallway are all features of this student-led program. According to CARA's other codirector, Lori Chajet, the youth who run peer programs embody this college-going identity through their work with their peers. As one of their youth described it, "As a youth leader . . ., I keep students on track and make sure they complete the right steps on time. Because I am also a student, we are in class together, in lunch together, and walking the same hallways. I use all of those times to remind students about what they need to be doing for college."

Some people might be reluctant to have young people leading this work that carries such high stakes—college attendance or even well-being. However, Bloom argues that it takes only one opportunity observing these young people in action to convince people otherwise.

One common concern that I have heard about peer counseling programs is that youth should not shoulder personal burdens that should instead be handled by trained counseling professionals.[25] However, scholars who have evaluated peer education programs suggest that training can make a big difference in whether a peer is ready to step into this role. Therefore, schools that wish to employ peer education or mentorship programs should ensure these initiatives are run under the supervision of a school counselor and provide thoughtful training for peer leaders.

The American School Counselor Association (ASCA) endorses the implementation of peer support programs in schools. As outlined in its

School Counselor and Peer Support Programs policy statement, peer support initiatives can bolster the effectiveness of school counseling programs through increasing the outreach of a counseling office and raising awareness of its available services.[26] Peer support programs can take a number of different forms including peer counseling and peer mentoring. Although the literature on peer counseling is limited, published work suggests that these programs have positive effects on the peer counselors, enhancing interpersonal skills such as active listening and communication.[27]

Counselors can draw on students' unique influence on other students when it comes to programming for younger children too. From reading programs to buddy programs, elementary school counselors can collaborate with middle and high school counselors and their own upper elementary students to deliver support services, raise postsecondary aspirations, and model and discuss hard work and effort. One practice that has recently gained popularity is the "senior walk," in which high school seniors dress up in their caps and gowns and parade through the elementary schools they attended to showcase what is in store for those young children. These kinds of experiences are great for students—giving them a chance to reflect on how far they've come and to be empowered as role models—while also supporting the work of school counselors.

Another powerful example of leveraging student leadership to share some of counselors' duties is student-led conferences. One reason that this approach is gaining in popularity is that educators have begun to see how giving students agency to facilitate these meetings provides an ideal opportunity for students to practice important life skills such as planning, reflecting, and taking initiative. Toby Marston, the counselor who spearheaded advisories in his school, also experienced success with giving students' ownership over student-led conferences.

At Mount Baker High School, students in grade nine through grade eleven lead conferences with their parents/family members. This student-led initiative was built into the advisory program, which means it is facilitated by teachers who lead classroom advisories. This fifteen-minute conference about how students are doing in school provides an opportunity for relationship building between school and home, while providing a platform for a conversation about school. From calling the parent and scheduling the appointment to leading the discussion, students take the lead. While the general focus of the conference is about how students are doing in school, these conferences are not limited to grades. They discuss classes, student progress and achievements, and even noncognitive skill development such as organization. These conferences, which take place in the spring, provide an important springboard for planning for the following year. According to Marston, parents attend about 75 percent of the conferences.

Because of the success of these sessions, the school has added a fall conference for incoming ninth graders to assist with the transition to high school. Marston proposed this idea to the leadership team that, knowing the research on the importance of ninth-grade success to school achievement, was quick to endorse the idea. Because of the trust built from the other data-driven initiatives, Mount Baker teachers were also excited about the expansion of this initiative.

Giving students the space to take this level of responsibility is certainly a risky endeavor, and for that reason, many educators are reluctant to put students in this type of leadership position. Some fear that too much is riding on these conversations to risk a student blowing it. However, Marston feels otherwise. "Even if a kid is 100 percent unprepared, it turns into a conversation about why he is unprepared." In other words, if supports are in place for students to successfully lead and they struggle, that experience gives educators powerful data about what additional skills warrant attention.

The growing interest in student-led conferences provides useful insight about how to begin this type of practice. Advocates of student-led conferences suggest starting small—even letting students attend or contribute in small ways to meetings or conferences.[28] Also, inviting students to lead these conferences means giving them time to prepare, building in scaffolds such as practice speaking about their strengths and challenges, and providing prompts to spur reflections about their past experiences or future goals.

One final example of how counselors can engage youth in their networks of support is through partnering with them to gather research about their school or youth experiences, notably known as Youth Participatory Action Research (YPAR). YPAR is a methodology rooted in participatory action research, a group process that brings together community members to identify and study issues related to a community's needs and experiences.[29] As its name suggests, YPAR focuses specifically on youth; by providing youth with an opportunity to explore, through a critical lens, issues affecting their lives, YPAR is a source of youth empowerment.[30] This approach is rooted in notions of justice, opening the eyes of youth to the production of injustice while simultaneously promoting forms of resistance that are necessary to produce social change.[31]

While counselors do not widely use YPAR as a tool for promoting student development or empowerment, there are some promising models in community agencies.[32] In one example of a yearlong YPAR project undertaken by two school counseling graduate students at a high school, the counselors saw firsthand the multiple benefits of this approach. In this example, graduate student interns met with nine students for two hours on a weekly basis, focusing initial conversations on brainstorming potential research topics, as well as discussing how and by whom knowledge is created.[33] The YPAR team eventually chose a project centering on a needs-based assessment of teen health and wellness. This project not only led to the development of a health and wellness class but also increased the YPAR participants' confidence and aspirations for pursuing higher education. Counselors may wish to partner with teachers to implement YPAR projects in specific classrooms as one way of giving students this space to lead.

Whether students use their lunches to connect with peers about future planning or use advisories to get trained in peer education programs, educators can enlist students in many ways to help with counseling practices to benefit all students. In practice, educators must be creative with timing and scheduling, and mindful about confidentiality and the importance of training. Nonetheless, the possibilities are there. Fortunately, we can learn a lot from the organizations that have allowed students to take the lead in areas typically carried out only by counselors.

GETTING AND STAYING CONNECTED

More than a strong network of people is needed to enact the academic home approach. School counselors and their partners also need to pay attention to *how* they will work together to ensure they are aligned and working in concert with one another and to avoid fragmentation of services. Drawing on the experiences of the medical profession that achieved increased access to health care with the medical home model, researchers determined that major barriers to implementing medical homes included training specialists in the medical home concept and communication and care coordination among multiple partners. Fortunately, we can learn a lot from the lessons learned from the medical model to ensure that school counselors who wish to enact an academic home attend to these important elements.

Just as educators often conceive of schools as hubs, coordinating supports for students in a given community, we can imagine school counselors operating in an academic home acting as a hub of a student's educational experience. As leaders of an academic home experience, school counselors coordinate comprehensive supports to set up students for success in school and life. They accomplish this goal by managing a wide array of stakeholder contributions to ensure coordination of care and avoid duplication of services that can sometimes mean fewer students are served. Drawing links between successful practices associated with the medical home and innovative school counseling efforts, I recommend that schools incorporate the use of strategic communication, teams, and partnership tools to create clear role definitions, clarity of purpose, and systems that support coordination of multiple partners.

Communication

The ability of school counselors to assume revised roles in schools hinges a great deal on their partners having updated expectations of their role. School counselors need to be able to communicate their unique role and purpose to many constituents. However, counselors also need to communicate expectations for how they intend to collaborate with teachers and school staff, families, students, and community organizations. While communication is certainly everyone's responsibility, the success of a coordinated system depends on counselors' commitment to establishing and maintaining this communication.

A strong communication plan includes a process for articulating counselors' role to students and their families. In one of the few studies exploring parent perceptions of counselors, educational researcher Dana Gillilan found that only half of the parents in her study believed their elementary school counselors were a valuable resource.[34] Other studies about parental perceptions of counselors reveal that parents have little understanding of how counselors spend their time. For example, in one study on parents' perception of counselors' role in college advising, researchers found that parents significantly overestimated the amount of personal and interpersonal counseling their students receive.[35] By contrast, these same families underestimated the amount of contact time devoted to proctoring assessments. Perhaps because of misperceptions about counselors' skill set and training, families from the same study also perceived school counselors to be a less credible source for information on college planning than college admission counselors, friends, and relatives.

One simple strategy for improving communication is making sure counseling departments are included and easily accessible on school websites. Surprisingly, that is not always the case. In their study of schools' online presence, researchers Aviva Shimoni and Lori Greenberg found that school counseling departments are not always included in school websites. In some cases, counselors were not identified personally or professionally, and the websites did not include information about the scope of school counselors' roles.[36] Creating a school counseling website that highlights the counseling department, the range of available support services available, and the best way to engage with the department is one way to communicate this important information. When parents and other involved family members have a clear expectation of school counselors, and, specifically, the role they play in coordinated supports for their child, counselors can better engage families as partners in productive ways.

Most school counselors value the importance of family engagement and strive to form strong partnership with families. Although counselors report wishing they had more time to work with families, most dedicate a portion of their time to talking with parents about student progress and, when necessary, conveying disciplinary infractions. Certainly, this effort constitutes a form of communication. Although these types of conversations are one way to build relationships, they rarely convey counselors' specific *role*. As a result, families' understanding of school counselors' functioning is limited to the circumstances they are working on, which for some families may never happen during a child's educational career.

Instead, school counselors and schools should ensure counselors' information, goals, and yearly programming plans are communicated with parents through school websites, written materials, and personal communication. Back-to-school nights and orientation programs where counselors typically discuss resources for students might incorporate more of a "What we do" session for families. Doing so can create a strong foundation for the much-needed collaborative work to bolster the support network provided by the academic home.

Like families, students would also benefit from a clarified vision of what their school counselors offer. When students see their counselors as partners in supporting their school experience, they are more likely to reach out if they find themselves in need of support. Yet too often, negative perceptions of school counselors send the message that counselors are too busy or unable to help. Such depictions undermine counselors' effectiveness by creating low expectations of counselors that deter students, families, educational partners, and leaders from leveraging all that school counselors have to offer. This point surfaced recently following the release of the controversial Netflix television series *13 Reasons Why*. Based on the young adult novel by Jay Asher, the show tells the story of seventeen-year-old Hannah Baker, who, before ending her life, sends a total of thirteen cassette tapes, one to each person who wronged her in some way. Each tape tells the story of someone or something that caused her to want to take her life. The final tape is sent to Mr. Porter, the school counselor to whom she reaches out in a final attempt to seek support for being bullied and raped, among other mistreatments. The tape illustrates how Hannah's last attempt for help, seeking support from her school counselor, contributes to her taking her own life. Among the many criticisms of this show and its depiction of suicide, school counselors questioned the implications of portraying a clueless, overburdened, and unhelpful school counselor. Counselors argued that this portrayal was detrimental to students and perhaps even unethical. Many criticized the producer's choice to portray a school counselor's response as unaware of the signs of suicide (which is very rare), unwilling to report an issue of abuse (all counselors are mandated reporters), and unhelpfully encouraging the student to "move on." Counselors and psychologists accused the producers of sending the message to struggling students that counselors can't help them. Phyllis Alongi, the clinical director of the Society for the Prevention of Teen Suicide, says she cringed when she saw that the show intentionally wrote the counselor to be ineffective and not at all representative of the many counselors her organization trains.[37] How are parents and students to form an expectation that someone in their school is there to help them when media portrayals suggest otherwise?

Certainly, school counselors are not responsible for media portrayals of their profession; however, they can take an active role in promoting students' understanding by signaling to students what they can expect when they approach their counselor or respond to offers of support. Broadcasting this message early and often in students' educational experiences can ensure that students are reminded of sources of support, often just in time. Schools can use bulletin boards, create pamphlets, communicate their role during orientations, and invite students to become ambassadors for counseling programs and services. For example, during sixth- or ninth-grade orientations, school counselors might describe their role, how to make an appointment, where to find their counselor, and how counselors work as a team with others to support students. Letting students know that counselors work as a team reinforces their role as a primary point of entry and will likely ensure that students reach out even if they are not certain their counselor can help.

One school in Connecticut found that by communicating some of its achievements, the counseling department also communicated to colleagues their mission. In this example, the school counselors embarked on a pilot project to improve attendance that included school counselors conducting home visits. With permission from the school principal, the four counselors visited the homes of students with a pattern of tardiness or absences. By the end of the year, the attendance rates increased significantly. Feeling proud of themselves and their students, the school counselors posted flyers indicating the increases in attendance. To their surprise, many colleagues expressed their appreciation for having a better understanding of what counselors did.

Responsibility for understanding school counselors' role falls on everyone working in a school, not just counselors. In her trainings with school districts, counselor educator Trish Hatch engages student support staff in an exercise about knowing one's "lane." In this exercise she invites school counselors, school social workers, school psychologists, and outside partners to discuss one another's role and how they function in their lane and in collaboration with others. Unsurprisingly, she routinely finds that the participants have a lot of role confusion and misunderstandings about one another's roles. This lack of clarity is frustrating for everyone involved, and worse, it reduces opportunities for successfully drawing on one another's expertise.

It is important for counselors to utilize formal measures for communicating with school leaders, staff, and families, instead of just hoping these parties will directly observe and recognize their value. An academic home framework creates time, space, and methods for this kind of communication, and that in turn can enable counselors to do their jobs successfully so students can learn successfully.

Team Building

Operating an academic home structure with a network of partners requires that counselors lead that network. One way for counselors to coordinate student care is to utilize teams that focus on a particular domain or developmental need. In US high schools, using teams is part of a larger trend of establishing student support teams (SST), composed of school staff that provide early, systematic assistance to students exhibiting behavioral or academic problems.[38] The SST (also sometimes known as a student intervention team) is a completely student-centered problem-solving team composed of educators who support the work of teachers and counselors to promote student achievement.[39] It builds on existing services and programs to enhance an institution's ability to respond to student needs.[40] Schools accomplish this by using a referral system that enables teachers and other school staff to refer students in need of additional support. The most prevalent supports offered by SSTs include monitoring student academic progress (Tier 1), creating tailored intervention plans (Tier 2), and referring students to intervention services (Tier 3).[41]

Teams, which may be composed of counselors, teachers, administrators, school nurses, school psychologists, and community social service agencies, work collaboratively to identify appropriate interventions or support services for struggling students. Recent data from the *National Survey on High School Strategies Designed to Help At-Risk Students Graduate* found that nearly 75 percent of high schools had student support teams in place; small schools as well as those located in urban areas were the most likely to institute such supports.[42] In the 2014–15 school year, approximately one in every six US high school students received assistance through a student support team.[43]

School counselors can also lead teams to promote students' postsecondary development, especially when a school has many partners and staff sharing responsibility for this domain. For example, a counselor might oversee a postsecondary leadership team composed of both school-based and community-based staff, and meet monthly with the whole team, facilitating each partner's sharing of progress and challenges. The Office of College and Career Success in the Chicago Public Schools has employed this approach of using postsecondary teams. It defines a postsecondary leadership team as a "body that drives a structured system of support that fosters a strong college-going culture and improved student postsecondary outcomes."[44] Composed of counselors, college and career coaches or advisors, principals, teachers, students, community partners and agencies, and even parents, postsecondary leadership teams utilize data-driven decision-making to shape a culture of success within schools. These teams also review data on postsecondary metrics to assess progress and identify gaps in services. With these kinds of teams in place, schools are better suited to promote the academic and personal development of students as well as to increase their college and career awareness, readiness, access, and success.[45]

As this Chicago model shows, postsecondary leadership teams reflect the coordination of comprehensive care that is essential to an academic home framework. Data is at the center of postsecondary teams. Information about students' progress on early indicators is used to inform the development and assessment of interventions that target student success. For example, the team might review data showing the number of students participating in a college fair, the percentage completing the FAFSA, or student enrollment in postsecondary education and ultimately persisting. Qualitative data about students' attitudes and beliefs, including the perceptions of students and their families concerning college affordability and access, are also critical in providing full context about the student experience at particular schools.

As a part of the High School College Access for All (CA4All) initiative in New York City, many schools are experimenting with postsecondary teams. This initiative seeks to close the gap between graduation and postsecondary enrollment by strengthening individual schools' capacity to create a college-going culture. As a part of CA4All, the New York City Department of Education Office of Postsecondary Readiness deploys a team of college coaches that work with cross-functional teams at various schools.[46] Through their work with coaches, the team uses data to engage in learning and idea development, often based on problems of practice identified by team members. These kinds of teams can set postsecondary goals for their students, identify gaps in programming at the school level, and develop strategies to widen access to postsecondary readiness. Like other student-focused teams, postsecondary or college-going culture teams reflect the need for network partners to work collaboratively with counselors using data.

In addition to these aforementioned teams, school counselors also lead transition teams to address what has become a growing need to support students both before and throughout the transition between elementary, middle, and high school. Using teams at this important juncture is especially important. Not only are students moving into a new environment, but they also are doing so at a developmental stage in which adolescents are facing innumerable cognitive, physical, and emotional changes. Plenty of evidence suggests that smooth transitions set up students for successful school experiences, and counselors can use transition teams to engage teachers, administrators, family members, and community partners to support those transitions. Together, this team can plan programming that is locally relevant and responsive to the unique needs of a class of students.

One of the benefits of using teams to realize an academic home approach to school counseling is that it provides a structure to other aspects of the home, such as distributive counseling. For example, a school counselor might oversee a team focused on social emotional learning, which might include a lead teacher who coordinates with the other teachers on implementing a universal SEL program in classrooms, along with the assistant principal who often deals with disruptive behavior, and mental health providers who help bolster the skills of students struggling with behavior challenges. Importantly, school counselors can take responsibility for overseeing all of the teams and would coordinate with the principal and other school leaders to ensure they are aligned with other schoolwide goals.

Partnership Tools

Anyone who has been part of a partnership knows that it takes work. Earlier in my career, I led an intermediary partnership organization that brought school districts together with university partners. One university president expressed his appreciation for our work, noting that most people fail to attend to the "muckety muck" that keeps partnerships going. Indeed, partnerships depend on systems to keep on track when things get busy. One way to accomplish this is to use tools that can create structure for the partnership. Memoranda of understanding (MOU) and orientation and onboarding discussions are two examples of tools that can help keep collaborative work on target.

When schools set out to partner with outside agencies, creating an MOU is a formal way to articulate and document how the partnership will work. Generally, an MOU is an agreement between two people or organizations that outlines how they will work together; it is less formal than a traditional contract and not legally binding. Dave Lewis, a school counselor from KIPP (Knowledge Is Power Program), a charter school in Massachusetts that serves students in educationally underserved communities, has used MOUs effectively to ensure not only that expectations among partners are clear but also that the needs of both schools and community partners are met.

As a school counselor, Dave Lewis works hard to find organizations that meet his students' various needs that can't be met in their school structure. While he sometimes builds informal relationships with community partners, he also utilizes MOUs in formal partnerships to ensure that each partner "can genuinely communicate what each program wants and needs from one another." For example, Lewis's school was partnering with a highly collaborative organization that wanted students to be dismissed early on certain days to meet the program requirements. Although the school was initially reluctant to make this accommodation, it also realized doing so was an important compromise for the partnership and one that was respectful and responsive to the school's needs. In this case, Lewis and the community partners included a stipulation in the MOU that approved students to leave early on select days to attend the program. As a result, Lewis has a positive relationship with the program director and personally advocates for students who need or would uniquely benefit from the program. The MOU communicates the trust that each organization has in the other and what they are willing to give to honor that relationship. Lewis also manages another strong partnership that began with three students from the high school attending the program on their own time and now includes a large group of students serving as peer leaders and the organization regularly coming to the school to connect with students, running workshops, and becoming part of the school community.

When counselors build authentic partnerships with community agencies, the MOUs support their academic home by documenting expectations and aligning other assets in the network. These informal agreements provide more than an avenue for communicating expectations; they also provide a vehicle for conversations about how things are going in the partnership, allowing for tweaks and modifications to be made if things go awry. They also provide documentation that counselors can use to review all their partnerships and continue to keep track of who does what. Although some partnerships certainly function quite well without an MOU, having this structure in place does not hurt, and more often than not, it helps.

Another best practice partnership tool that bolsters school counselors' ability to successfully connect outside agencies to schools and students is the use of orientations or launch events. Using an orientation to bring together various partners or staff working on a similar area provides the foundation for a strong working relationship. Furthermore, these partners need to understand the culture of the school and how their work can enhance the good work already underway. To accomplish this, school counselors might offer an orientation or even a yearly meeting with outside partners. Toby Marston from Mount Baker High School knows that early orientations go a long way toward building a collaborative team.

Marston meets with all of his outside providers every fall. In fact, he asks his out-of-school partners to bring their supervisors. These fall meetings include presentations and discussions about goals the school is working toward, such as attendance. These meetings provide the opportunity for people to "realize they are not working in isolation" and reinforce, where possible, other initiatives going on in schools.

An important aspect of early orientation is the opportunity to highlight what is already being done in a particular area, which only helps organizations become better partners. I recall an instance early in my career when I was called into a meeting with my school principal to meet representatives from a new program that aspired to work in our school with students. The director of this new initiative began the conversation with an assurance that this new program would "complement existing efforts." This comment struck me as odd. I wondered, "How do they know what we are doing?" As leaders of coordinated services, school counselors need to take the time to communicate with external partners about the promising work already going on so that their efforts may indeed "complement existing efforts." Annual orientations or launch events provide an opportunity to bring community partners to the school to support relationship building and build trust, as well as discuss processes to ensure a collaborative and meaningful experience for students.

KEEPING THE NETWORK HEALTHY

Similar to collective impact, where community coalition building is used to address intractable community issues, academic homes function best when the network is healthy. Collective impact models stress the importance of backbone supports that facilitate the work across the coalition. In a similar way, school counselors provide that backbone support in schools. When they are able to provide leadership in developing and managing academic homes, counselors are better positioned to leverage the contributions of their teachers, school, and community partners. Given the growing number of partner programs and agencies—especially given dwindling school budgets and the need for community and university resources—this kind of leadership is more than nice to have; it is essential for counselors and students to succeed.

4

⬩⬩

OPPORTUNITIES
FOR SCHOOL LEADERS

Sharing Responsibility for Student Success

At TechBoston Academy in Boston, Massachusetts, the school counseling department uses "intervention teams" to identify and support students for whom teachers or other staff have concerns. The idea for these teams emerged following a conversation between Jillian Kelton, the school's lead counselor, and her colleague, the director of special education. After one student support team meeting during which student support referrals were discussed, the two women agreed that they needed a more structured approach to identify and support struggling students. Although it was helpful to have teachers grouped together to discuss student cases that often led to a referral, Kelton knew that the school needed a uniform approach to case conferencing that engaged other student support providers, such as the nurse or school mental health clinician. Kelton brought this emerging idea for a new structure to one of her school's coprincipals and received enthusiastic support for the intervention team idea.

The coprincipal not only got behind the idea of a new team but also wanted to participate! Despite the demands of running a large school, one of the school's two leaders has attended team meetings ever since. In consultation with teachers, family members, and colleagues who know a given student well, counselors gather information about that student to bring to intervention team meetings. Counselors collect information such as the student's strengths, school history, attendance, testing scores, and a list of previously tried interventions.

The principals' engagement with this team has been invaluable. Having a school principal (and sometimes assistant principal too) on the team brings a unique lens to student case discussions. The principals are more tuned into the key issues facing the students and the school, and sometimes they play a key role in the action plan for follow-up. For example, at the conclusion of one case conference regarding a tenth-grade boy whose behaviors were consistent with youth who have experienced trauma, one administrator noted that according to the data he was keeping, this was the fourth case in which incidences of trauma or behaviors consistent with traumatic backgrounds were present. Together, the team made an action plan to request professional development for the entire school staff on the topic of student trauma. The principal thought this was an important action step to ensure that the student and others like him encounter teachers and support staff who understand the impact of trauma and recognize the warning signs as they present in schools.

Kelton believes that these intervention teams would not exist if her school leader had not given her the authority and room to create and lead this kind of initiative. Perhaps more importantly, Kelton knows that the principal's attendance and deep engagement with intervention teams keep their work integrated into the school's vision and planning, which helps both the counselors and students alike.

What is happening at TechBoston Academy is an example of what happens when schools place counselors in leadership roles and enable them to organize, manage, and deliver support services in collaboration with their partners. At the school, counselors are already operationalizing many aspects of an academic home approach because they are supported by a school leader who sees them as partners who are instrumental to the school's academic mission. They are viewed as experts on their students, and although they may not directly deliver all the counseling supports, they play a leadership role that capitalizes on their strong relationships with students and the contributions of their colleagues. Importantly, the TechBoston Academy counselors have also enacted a key tenet of an academic home: a support team. The counselors credit their positive experience to working for school leaders who have appropriate and high expectations for what counselors do. In turn, these expectations shape administrative decisions regarding everything from caseload assignments to hiring practices. As such, the counselors at this sixth- to twelfth-grade school experience working conditions that position them to effectively do their jobs.

School leaders, especially principals and assistant principals, are some of the most important stakeholders in successful counseling programs, even though they may not typically see themselves in such a role. School leaders are usually responsible for hiring, supervising, and evaluating counselors, and for school counselors to create the kinds of academic homes that will set up students for success, effective school principal-school counselor relationships are essential. School leaders are essential to setting the conditions for counselors to operationalize aspects of the academic home approach, and that requires they develop a clear vision of how counselors can help schools meet their academic, social emotional, and postsecondary goals.

Unfortunately, the experience at TechBoston Academy is not universal, and as a result, some students miss out on the supports that come from counselors using the tools they know can work. Too many schools do not have the systems or even the expectations of counselors to lead or manage in this way. If school leaders want to set up their counselors to provide students an academic home, they need to have a clear understanding of what counselors can do, the impact they can have on education, and the system and supports that enable them to be effective. In this chapter, I describe the importance of school leaders forming strong relationships with counselors, their aligning counseling with schoolwide improvement efforts, and their clarity about the kinds of roles that leaders should (and should not) expect counselors to assume. I illustrate how school leaders can take action steps toward creating the conditions necessary for counselors to positively influence students' educational experiences, including appropriate caseloads, counselor assignments, responsibilities, and professional development.

SETTING GREAT (AND UPDATED) EXPECTATIONS

A prerequisite to school counseling programs applying the academic home approach is the presence of leaders who have a fundamental belief in the purpose of counseling and support programs. The counselors at TechBoston Academy know that their school leaders fully understand their unique contributions to student achievement, which enables them to develop, implement, and manage the intervention team. The importance of such a belief may be obvious, but it cannot be taken for granted. Despite growing research on the connection between academic, social, and emotional learning, not all educators or leaders have had the chance to develop this lens. As one principal described to me when I asked him what makes for an effective school counseling program:

> There has to be a fundamental belief that if you're going to improve what happens academically, you need to tend to the social and emotional needs of your students. That's not just for kids who are in crisis, but that's true for kids who don't know how to set goals [for example]. There's a big umbrella of that work that needs to be done in order to increase the potential for better academic work. If you don't believe that, then you're not going to do that work as it relates to guidance.

Like most professionals, school counselors will be better at their jobs if their supervisors hold high expectations for what they can accomplish. And when school leaders understand what counselors are capable of doing, they will depend on them to take the kinds of initiative that schools need to be successful. A principal at a school with a strong counseling program and department described his counselors in this way:

> We have a lot of self-starters, so they'll come up with an idea and they'll run with it. Whether it's redo the transition to college program we do for our seniors, or we adopted a Signs of Suicide, SOS program, to work with the seventh and ninth grade. The counselors—give them something; they'll grab it and go with it.

I have witnessed far too many school leaders who feel that their counselors are underperforming but don't realize that their school structures and systems hamstring those counselors. This kind of perspective is not surprising given the lack of understanding between these two groups of professionals. Too often school leaders have not been trained in how to work with their counselors. To remedy this situation, school leaders can and should work with counselors to establish schoolwide goals across academic, social emotional, and postsecondary domains.

Promoting Principal-Counselor Alliances

Scratch the surface of a highly productive counseling program and you will usually find a strong relationship between the principal and counselors. With strong visions and relationships in place, school counselors can use their skills and understanding of students to help bring their vision to fruition.

In 2008, the National Association of Secondary School Principals (NASSP), American School Counselor Association (ASCA), and the College Board teamed up to examine the aspects of the principal-counselor relationship that are most essential to student success. Based on their survey of strong counselor-principal relationships, they identified three areas as fundamental to a strong relationship: mutual trust and respect, principal-counselor communication, and shared vision and decision-making.[1] Not surprisingly, school leaders and counselors effectively partner together when they have a shared understanding of appropriate roles and expectations. Conversely, low expectations and lack of support for school counselors can be partially traced to misperceptions among school leaders, educators, parents, and the general public regarding what counselors do and how they influence student achievement.

School principals and counselors report that communication is critical to ensure that collaborative relationships are developed and clear expectations are conveyed.[2] Examples of positive principal-counselor relationships illustrate that the quality of relationships increases when they work as a team, communicate a shared vision, and utilize frequent structured meetings to share decision-making and implementation of new programs.[3] For example, in some schools, counselors meet weekly with the school leader, often discussing data. In other cases, counselors are members of the leadership team and, as a result, have clear paths of communication with school administrators.

A common element of positive principal-counselor relationships is the use of annual agreements. Annual agreements provide a structured tool to communicate expectations such as how counselors will spend their time and what goals will drive their work.[4] For example, in a given year, a school counseling department might set three goals that address attendance, math achievement, and school safety. Accompanied by goal metrics in which counselors and leaders set targets for counselors' work, the agreement also documents how counselors will dedicate their time to activities that are aimed to meet those goals. These agreements are a good way to set a clear agenda aligned with the school's yearly goals. Organizations such as ASCA and even many school districts have templates that can be used by schools that want to adopt this practice.[5]

Defining the Role of Counselors

As school leaders formulate their expectations of counselors' roles, they need to understand the value of counselors providing support across multiple domains. As most school counselors will tell you, their work does not necessarily fall neatly into one domain; they support academic outcomes, social emotional development, and postsecondary opportunities, and those domains overlap. Counselors' efforts in one domain have the potential to bring about better outcomes in another. Just as we know that when kids eat a healthy breakfast, they are better able to learn, we also know that when students have access to support for personal stressors, they are better able to engage in their classes and perform well on tests. Similarly, when adults understand students' learning styles, they can provide students the accommodations they need, and the students have more positive experiences at school and learn better. Trusting relationships formed with counselors set the foundation for students to seek support from counselors as new challenges develop.

The following is an example of a school leader's decision to integrate school counselors' roles and how this decision set the stage for a productive collaboration:

When Roberta began her position as a principal at a new high school, she knew she wanted to bring the integrated school counselor model from her old school. She began by restructuring the school counselors' roles to prioritize students' academic and social emotional development. She explained that she expected counselors to provide direct and responsive counseling to students on issues such as identity development, anxiety, and goal setting, while also implementing systemic interventions such as classroom-based lessons, training school staff, running counseling groups, and being a care coordinator for high need students. Because the counselors were trained in counseling and had recently felt that part of their role had become diminished, they were excited for the change.

With grant funding, Roberta also brought on three specialized college and career advisors who were hired to provide specific postsecondary programming and support. She created clear job descriptions that outlined their specific responsibilities, including early college and career-exposure activities and instrumental support planning for postsecondary opportunities. She was clear in her expectations that the school counselors and college and career advisors would work together to support students through an articulation of roles. She had been part of a similar model at her previous school and knew that, with the right structures and expectations in place, it could work well for students.

Jake, one of the counselors at Roberta's school, loved the collaborative aspect of his work with the new college and career advisors in the new system. He quickly found that their professional roles naturally intersected and credits the time Roberta asked them to spend crafting communication and team structures with helping to make this happen. Despite no longer helping students with the instrumental tasks associated with college planning, he appreciated the focus of his role promoting students' postsecondary development in new ways. In his case, Jake provided developmental supports to prepare students to understand their identities and what they wish to do with their lives, acted as a resource in decision-making processes, communicated with families, and helped students understand when a traditional schooling model was not right for them and found them an alternative placement. Also, by looping with the same grade for all four years of high school, Jake developed deep relationships with his students, which positioned him to help students think about their futures while leveraging the unique assets of the school's college and career advisors who ran classroom workshops and seminars to provide early college awareness and planning support.

By the end of her second year, Roberta was pleased with how the model was beginning to take shape. An unintended benefit of this restructure was the increase in counselors' readiness and interest in tackling some system-level challenges, such as the lack of parent engagement. She knew this would require helping them find the right balance of systems change and direct service work. However, with the good work already underway, she excitedly set this as a goal for her third year.

It might not seem revolutionary to suggest that school leaders need to articulate their expectation that school counselors support students across all three domains, while articulating their relationship with other related staff roles. However, as the profession has evolved and counselors have found themselves adjusting their role to meet changing societal needs, educational leaders have not necessarily shifted their expectations of counselors over time. Whereas at one time administrators expected high school counselors to serve as registrars, focusing primarily on course selection, many now are slow to see them as college counselors. Yet in other schools, counselors are expected to focus only on barriers to learning. This shift has led to confusion on the part of school leaders as well as inaccurate perceptions of counselor competence. In the preceding example, new school leader Roberta created a vision that expected counselors to deliver supports across all three domains, while utilizing a different kind of staff support for post-high school planning. This approach reflects the comprehensive care tenet of an academic home approach.

Some educational leaders have questioned whether counselors have been adequately trained in mental health and psychopathology and whether they have the time to provide clinical supports. However, most school counselors are trained and positioned to conduct universal health screening, refer students to mental health counselors, educate teachers about mental health and education, and deliver classroom lessons on wellness and emotional health.

With a clearer understanding that counselors can and should work effectively across all three domains, school leaders will be better positioned to make decisions that support this approach. As a result, they can act in a way that conveys a clear expectation of school counselors and a vision for what they hope counselors will do. This vision will go a long way toward ensuring students have access to school counseling supports that are aligned with the school's goals.

Situating School Counseling in the School

When school leaders and counselors agree on how to promote student success, the school counseling program can more clearly fit into the broader mission of schooling. Along with counselors, teachers, nurses, custodians, administrators, and a host of support staff all aim to create educational spaces where students can learn and thrive. Where school counselors fit into this broader enterprise matters. This includes everything from office location to reporting relationships. Positioning school counseling programs optimally within the larger structure of a school building or mission will go a long way toward supporting the development of a coordinated academic home.

Where school counselors are housed, literally and figuratively, matters. Therefore, it is worth stepping back and considering some of these logistical aspects of school structures. For example, where counselors are located in a school can impact service delivery. In some schools, counselors work in a suite or area together, often with other role partners. In others, offices are located in specific parts of the building where they have access to their unique caseload. This is true in many large high schools where school counselors have offices in "houses" or small learning communities. Certainly, both models have merit, and space issues are often a challenge in schools. Consequently, counselors often are relieved to have private spaces at all. Yet, collaborative space is a priority when teams of people need to work together to support students. Therefore, when possible, school leaders should find ways to provide counselors the collaborative spaces for them to work together and align the web of supports necessary in an academic home approach.

Counselors' organizational place in a school also plays a part in their service delivery. Do school counselors report to a principal or a department chair? Who provides leadership for the counselors? In some schools, leadership comes from a director of school counseling, as in the case of TechBoston Academy. Others do not, especially at the elementary and middle school levels. Often school districts employ counseling directors or coordinators; however, this often depends on the size and type of school. Nevertheless, having someone at the school level who takes responsibility for aligning the school counseling program with a school-wide mission and goals and can participate on a leadership team matters significantly.

In schools that do not have directors or department chairs, leadership from within the school counseling department is key. A compromise to this approach is to identify someone as a lead counselor, giving this person added responsibility and perhaps a smaller caseload. This counselor can be empowered to lead the network, establish and manage strategic partnerships, assist with hiring, and advocate for policies that reduce barriers to learning for students and those that support a school counseling program. A lead counselor or director can also provide much-needed supervision, which is often difficult for school leaders with no training in this area.

One strategy to ensure that students have access to the kinds of supports that define an academic home approach is to place a school counselor, or a director if one exists, on the school's leadership team. The school leaders from TechBoston Academy utilized this approach and, according to its Director of Student Support and Counseling, is a central force behind why their intervention team has been so successful. As the counselors at that school shared, having a voice on the leadership team that represents the goals of the counseling department has created trust and understanding among the administrative team. As one counselor described to me, "From my perspective, the fact that [school administrators] both acknowledge the need for the kind of support we're providing and are 100 percent behind what we're doing, that makes a huge difference." When counselors feel supported and valued by their school leaders, that will go a long way toward their efficacy.

ENACTING AN ACADEMIC HOME VISION: LEADERSHIP ACTION STEPS

Certainly, making change takes more than having high expectations and alignment between administrators and a counseling department. School leaders' everyday decisions shape the context in which counselors carry out their work. This means supporting counselors as they strive to enact an academic home. This support can take many forms; however, it especially includes encouraging counselors to create meaningful mis-

109

sion statements, updating school counselors' job descriptions, reviewing professional duties, examining caseloads and student assignments, and ensuring access to high-quality professional development.

Supporting School Counseling Mission Statements

For an academic home approach to deliver the types of supports that help students succeed, school counselors need to be included in the broader mission of the school. In some places, including them means schools adopt mission statements explicitly stating the developmental aspect of schooling. In other places, this might mean that school counseling programs create mission statements that situate their work within the larger educational vision of the school. Addressing both of these strategies is necessary for school counselors to ensure their work is advancing both specific student needs and larger schoolwide goals.

School mission statements provide direction and clear signaling of the core values of the school. They convey a school's philosophy and specific goals for enacting that philosophy. Some might argue that those statements are more marketing than true value statements, but ultimately the mission statement is the only explicit articulation of a school's values. Most school mission statements emphasize giving students skills to become "lifelong learners," "productive citizens," or "responsible citizens in a global community." In this way, mission statements already reflect a primary aim of school counseling programs: the postsecondary readiness aspect. Where these mission statements sometimes fall short, however, is attention to human development. For example, most schools value the importance of providing a safe, caring, and supportive school climate. However, those values are often missing from school vision or mission statements. To better situate school counseling as central to that mission, school mission statements should reflect a commitment to supporting students' personal development, as well as their academic and postsecondary development. Not only is this an accurate way to reflect a school's mission, but it also makes all stakeholders, counselors included, excited about bringing that mission to fruition.

School counseling programs also need specific mission statements that represent their internal core values and purposes; in fact, ASCA suggests that all school counseling programs establish a mission statement that drives their programming. According to ASCA, school counseling mission statements should align with the school mission statement so that counseling programs employ programs and practices that help schools achieve schoolwide goals. Typically, these statements should define the scope of counselors' efforts, emphasize whom they aim to serve (all students!), and identify key partners, such as family and community members, for whom the services are intended.[6] Some schools use these statements to signal the vast network of professionals who work together to deliver support services. In enacting a key aspect of the academic home vision, school counselors might also emphasize the student-centered aspect and the network of collaborators and specialists who will work together to promote the intended outcome, which is likely student success.

Here's how mission statements can make a big difference:

When Traci Small arrived at Somerville High School in Massachusetts as the new school counseling director, she immediately set out to create a mission statement for the counseling department. After several years as a school counselor and director at a school in a different state, she knew that mission statements had played a key role in her professional experience. When she began her new position as director, she encountered a department that was floundering and in desperate need of an identity. Drawing on her past experience, Small knew that getting students to access counselors and their programming depended on publicizing to others what counselors do. Too often, she argued, school counselors' roles were a mystery to teachers, administrative staff, and parents.

Together with the counselors, Small set out to create a brochure that articulated the school counseling department's identity, purpose, and mission to support students. By gathering feedback from multi-

ple counselors and role partners in the school, she was able to create a coherent statement about what the counseling department does and what programs and services it offered to achieve that mission. Today, that mission is captured in a brochure shared with various stakehold-ers, represented in the school's Department Spotlight, a video cre-ated by the broadcasting class, and even T-shirts that were made to emphasize that the school's seven counselors are "school counselors" and not "guidance counselors."

The brochure, which has been translated into multiple languages, is used internally and externally. Internally, Small finds that teach-ers have a better understanding of what the counselors do and, as a result, reach out when they need support with a particular student or group of students. Externally, it is used with parents and family members, as well as community partners who wish to work with the school. Small found that the brochure and the messages it contains have been very helpful with community partners who support stu-dents' college readiness and mental health. It gives them "a framework for how our school works and who works in our department. It sets them up to be better partners because they understand what we are trying to accomplish."

While some readers might think that developing a brochure is a rather elementary idea, it turns out that this relatively small step goes a long way. According to Traci Small, the process of developing the mission and communicating it to colleagues helped give the department the identity it was missing. At times perceptions of the school's counselors were neg-ative. Some counselors felt that they were not respected members of the school. Together, these forces created a culture of distrust among coun-selors, administrators, and teachers. However, articulating and commu-nicating the department's mission helped professionalize the department and created a shared understanding of how counselors, administrators, and teachers shared responsibility for student success. This shift made counselors feel valued, which positively shapes their everyday actions with students.

Updating School Counseling Job Descriptions

Another way for school leaders to embark on a clarified role and expectations is through revised job descriptions. These descriptions should be created to show the scope of the work and aligned, where possible, with the mission of the school. With significant changes in the profession, many school counseling job descriptions need updating. One counselor who was hired in the past five years told me that she was hired with a job description that was written in the 1980s!

School leaders might work with school counselors to ensure that new positions and job descriptions accurately reflect the scope of counselors' efforts. Many models and examples available for review articulate specific roles, responsibilities, and even professional competencies that are expected.

Prioritizing School Counselors' Time with Students

Setting up counselors to deliver comprehensive, interconnected supports means ensuring that they have the time to develop programs, deliver counseling services, and capitalize on the contributions of others. Counselors routinely report spending over half of their time on noncounseling duties and desire more time in front of students and school staff. Many counselors agree that administrative duties are all part of being on a team and, importantly, can be a means to building relationships with students and other professionals. The problem, however, is that simply too many of these duties are given to counselors. With responsibilities from lunch duty and hallway duty to test administration, school counselors sometimes feel more like building aides than counselors. According to a study conducted by the National Association for College Admission Counseling (NACAC), counselors spend over 30 percent of their time on noncounseling duties—and administrators wish it was even more![7] A national report from the College Board found that nearly 20 percent of administrators would have their counselors spend "a lot more" or "a little more time" on administrative tasks in order to improve student success.[8] Clearly, administrators are struggling to fill these various tasks. However, when these duties are added to school counselors' plates, something else slides off—often something core to the goals of counseling and the school. What can be done? School leaders might ask teachers and paraprofessionals to pick up some of these duties or ask counselors to rotate these responsibilities so that they do not become onerous. For some school leaders, it might be helpful to have counselors track their schedule for a week to see just how much time they spend on counseling-related tasks versus other noncounseling duties.

For school leaders who need counselors to help with administrative duties, I recommend some compromises, especially in middle schools that sometimes have limited administrative staff. Sharing these responsibilities with other school staff, hiring paraprofessionals or retired staff, and demonstrating that school leaders also carry out these duties will go a long way toward reducing the number of duties counselors are given. However, school leaders might do other things such as purchasing a rolling cart so counselors can monitor students in high traffic areas while keeping up with some of their work.

Even if school leaders continue to use counselors for administrative duties, some of these duties actually run counter to counselors' goals and therefore undermine their efforts. Schools should avoid having counselors perform clerical work, cover classes, and execute disciplinary actions because these tasks can compromise the trust and relationship building that counselors are building with students. This was true for Jordan, a counselor in a high poverty school.

Jordan felt powerless. For the second year in a row, he and his counseling colleagues had been assigned a new duty—managing the metal detectors in the morning. Ever since the school laid off the discipline coordinator, the four school counselors had been told to staff the metal detectors several days a week. Without question, the worst part of the duty was searching a student's bag. Jordan felt that process directly undermined the trust he was trying to build with students. How was he going to get students to trust him if they saw him as a disciplinarian? He understood that the school was under-resourced and that fact initially drew him to the school; he knew his being there would make a difference. However, some days he felt it wouldn't matter if he didn't work there because he was not able to do much in the current setup.

A break came at an admissions open house when Jordan ran into another counselor he knew from graduate school. His classmate, Ana, described how she was using a computer program to track her hours and which students she was seeing as a means of illustrating how she was using her time. Ana explained how much her principal appreciated the additional information and that together they were working to reduce the number of administrative duties she was doing. Although things had not yet changed dramatically, she felt better knowing that her school leader was working in partnership with her to better understand and address the problem. Jordan left the event encouraged and excited to share the idea with his colleagues.

For principals, I recommend reflecting on the goals of the department and considering ways to evenly distribute responsibilities across the entire staff. Likewise, I suggest that leaders exercise caution when assigning duties and assign only those that are aligned with their counseling vision. Along with some of these changes, principals might also help their counselors see how some administrative duties can support their mission. For example, as a school counselor, I initially balked at being asked to do three lunch duties a day. I worried that spending one and a half hours in the lunchroom would limit my ability to reach students. However, I quickly found that I could accomplish quite a lot with students during that time. I could check in with students about ongoing issues, identify students who might not be connecting well with peers, and observe relationship patterns that would ultimately make their way to my office via a tearful student. More importantly, students knew who I was and thus were more likely to reach out to me. For other counselors, this might mean encouraging them to use hallway duty to hand out fly-ers or other materials that students need, or in elementary schools, use morning bus or drop-off duty to be the first point of contact in a student's day. At the least, school leaders might begin by engaging in a conversa-tion with counselors to see if they have concerns about any responsibili-ties that overwhelmingly take time away from counseling.

A word of caution about collective bargaining: some school counsel-ors use their collective bargaining as one way to advocate for fewer duties and changes in working conditions. Although these approaches can be helpful in certain situations, relying on contractual limits alone fails to communicate the real reason why being assigned so many duties is prob-lematic. Ultimately, counselors must advocate for their roles and meeting students' needs because performing these other duties takes counselors away from addressing students' needs. If this message isn't communi-cated, the result may be a short-term win but not lasting change in the way a school and its leaders understand and treat counseling.

Keeping Student-Counselor Caseloads at a Minimum

If counselors are to provide an academic home that balances systemic strategies with a comprehensive service delivery model, student-coun-selor caseloads must be kept as low as possible, as noted previously. According to a growing body of research, keeping caseloads down can have a remarkable effect on student achievement. Research on caseload size has found that lower student-counselor caseloads are associated with lower disciplinary rates, higher attendance, improved graduation rates, and increased likelihood of college enrollment.[9] In one study, educational researchers John Carey, Karen Harrington, Ian Martin, and Dawn Ste-venson examined school counseling programs in Utah and found that lower student-to counselor ratios were significantly associated with higher attendance rates and fewer disciplinary incidents.[10] In another study, College Board researchers Michael Hurwitz and Jessica Howell wanted to know whether the hiring of an additional school counselor would affect a school's four-year college-going rate. Using existing data from the National Center for Education Statistics' (NCES) Schools and Staffing Survey (SASS), these researchers found that, on average, each additional counselor is responsible for a ten-percentage point increase in a school's four-year college-going rate.[11] These data make a strong case for keeping counselor caseloads low.

Despite the fact that research tells us that smaller caseloads lead to improved student outcomes, however, many schools still maintain high caseloads.[12] In 1959, former Harvard University President James Conant published the groundbreaking book *The American High School Today*. In this comprehensive vision for public education, Conant recommended a student-to-counselor ratio of 250:1. This is still the optimal ratio recommended by ASCA and others in the field.[13] Yet, the national average remains at 443:1. Although these caseloads are based on data from the US Department of Education's National Center for Education Statistics, these statistics mask important differences by school type. For example, counselors working in schools educating high percentages of low-income students report even higher caseloads. In fact, only 4.2 percent of urban school districts meet the ASCA recommended guidelines with a ratio below 250:1.[14] Elementary school counselors tend to have much higher caseloads because districts tend to concentrate their counseling resources in high schools. Moreover, some counselors in rural areas are responsible for an entire school district; the small size of these districts sometimes means that counselors are more likely to have a ratio close to 250:1, but those counselors can lose precious face time with students when their time is spread across multiple schools.[15]

Further supporting the calls for lowering caseloads are studies showing that reductions in ratios have shown promising results. The School Counselor Corps Grant Program (SCCGP) is a Colorado state-funded initiative first launched in 2008 that increased the availability of effective school counseling in secondary institutions.[16] The program offered state funding to support the hiring of additional school counselors, along with professional development for counselors and program development activities such as Individual Career and Academic Plans (ICAP).[17] The aim of this program was to boost the graduation rate of Colorado high school students as well as the number of students who are prepared for, apply to, and ultimately matriculate at four-year postsecondary institutions.[18] Currently, three cohorts of schools have received funding, and so far, the outcomes are persuasive. Increases in on-time graduation rates and FAFSA completion rates point to a worthwhile investment in lowering student-counselor caseloads.

While it may be impossible for all schools to achieve the national average of one counselor for every 250 students, many schools can take steps to get closer to that average. The initiative underway in Colorado makes a compelling case for similar statewide investments; however, school leaders can also keep caseloads low by hiring additional counselors and avoiding cutting counselors during budgetary crises. Too often, tight budgets leave school leaders questioning the value of lowering caseloads in relation to other pressing needs. Yet, school leaders who understand the benefit of counseling programs to advance student achievement will be better equipped to make informed choices during tight times.

Examining Student-Counselor Assignments

Like caseload size, counselor assignments also play an important role in the continuity and coordination of care that is central to an academic home. The decision about how to assign students to a counselor may seem like a tedious, logistical aspect of the work, yet this is a question principals often ask me. The four most common ways to assign school counselors are by surname, grade level, teachers, and content specialization.

Most commonly, schools create counselor assignments based on students whose last names fall within a certain range of the alphabet, regardless of grade. Nationally representative data from the US Department of Education's High School Longitudinal Study (HSLS:09) show that about 59 percent of all public schools use this model.[19] Because siblings who share a last name are placed with the same counselor, this method can provide an opportunity for counselors to gain a meaningful understanding of students' family contexts.[20] Given the range of students within a caseload, this model also positions counselors to collaborate with teachers and other counseling staff to effectively address the diverse challenges facing students. Finally, this structure ensures that counselors can offer the continuity of care across multiple years in a given school, a key tenet of an academic home approach.

In some schools, students are assigned to their counselors based on grade level. The two forms of counselor assignment by grade level are static and looping. Whereas counselors in a static arrangement oversee students only in a particular grade, counselors in a looping assignment move with students across grade levels. One significant advantage of the static model is that counselors develop expertise with grade-specific and developmentally appropriate activities and strategies.[21] By contrast, the looping model supports counselors in establishing long-term relationships with students, which serve as a foundation for providing support on a wide range of issues. In my first year as a counselor, I was assigned to grade nine—a static assignment. While I relished the opportunity to focus my work on transition supports, early college awareness, and developmental competencies associated with early adolescence, all while working collaboratively with one set of teachers, I often felt that the strong relationships I formed with students were difficult to maintain as they moved on to the next grade and another counselor.

In other schools, counselor assignments are aligned with groups of teachers, meaning that counselors advise students enrolled in specific classes, teams of teachers, or a small learning community. Although this method supports the development of a strong student support system, it offers limited consistency as students change teachers, and thus counselors, each year.[22]

Finally, some assignments are based on specialization, with particular counselors taking responsibility for overseeing student development in specific areas such as career and college preparation, special education, or multicultural counseling. This approach was operationalized in one high school I visited as a counselor. This high school had a counselor for academic issues, one for personal issues, and one for postsecondary planning. After experimenting with this approach for several years, the school eventually moved to a surname assignment, recognizing that the limitations of inconsistent and fragmented support outweighed the benefit of specializing in a particular domain.

Although there is little research on the best way to assign students, there is good reason to believe that some models may be better than others. If counselors are going to provide continuity of care and build trusting relationships, they need to work across domains and with the same students over their entire educational careers.

Prioritizing Professional Learning and Development

When the school leaders from TechBoston Academy created and implemented the intervention team described at the beginning of this chapter, they were drawing on skills and knowledge related to using data, facilitating teams, understanding behaviors associated with trauma, and implementing a host of other competencies. Developing the skills and knowledge to implement a wide range of functions, from group counseling to leadership and advocacy, depends on strong preservice and in-service or professional development and training. However, school leaders play an important role in ensuring that counselors have access to relevant and timely professional development.

School leaders can and should make sure counselors make time for professional development and, when possible, dedicate resources to support those efforts. In my own research, I have found that financial and time constraints, as well as limited release time granted by school leaders, often stand in the way of counselors receiving professional development. Counselors routinely report that they are rarely given release time to attend trainings outside the school building, even when something is offered that would support their growth. However, according to one principal who heard me speak at a conference on this topic, "It's virtually impossible for us to send everybody out to something. [You've] got to have people here to cover. To send one representative to any meeting, we can do that." While closing an entire school counseling department for a full day can feel daunting to a high school leader, or any school leader, it sends a powerful message to adults and students alike about the importance of professional learning and the value of these professionals. When that is not possible, however, school leaders should ask counselors to take turns or send counselor teams so that counselors can learn new ideas together with a future collaborator.

One thing school leaders might do to remedy the time out of the building dilemma is to think differently and more deeply about what professional learning can look like. In other areas of education, new attention is moving toward job-embedded and sometimes personalized professional learning, rather than off-site trainings. The school counseling field has joined this movement with new webinars and online certificate programs. Of course, it is important for counselors to connect with other counselors, so off-site time is needed too. However, there is value—and the logistical benefit—to in-house support, mentoring, and training.

Another limiting factor to counselors' participation in professional development is cost. It makes sense that schools limit resources allocated to professional development that benefits only a small percentage of their staff. Yet, often school leaders are unaware of how existing federal funds could be used to support school counselors' professional development. During his time as US Secretary of Education, Arne Duncan penned a letter to school principals calling for them to "make wise investments in professional development for school counselors."[23] With this letter, the then secretary listed the major federal programs whose funds can be used to support school counseling programs, as well as professional development. Some of these federal programs included Title I, Elementary and Secondary School Counseling Programs, McKinney-Vento Education for Homeless Children and Youth Program, and School Improvement Grants.

In addition to supporting counselors' efforts to attend professional development outside their schools, school leaders can find ways to make the most of in-school professional development. In my time as a counselor, I attended far too many professional development sessions that were geared toward meeting the needs of teachers, who represent the majority of the staff. As was the case with me, counselors were asked to choose between learning about something that had only tangential relevance to their work or using the free time to catch up on paperwork and records. School principals might consider partnering with nearby schools to share the cost of bringing in an outside presenter or advocating for district resources to be used to offer relevant professional development for groups of counselors.

It is also important to note that counselors themselves can be a resource for providing professional development, not just for their colleagues, but for the entire staff. School-counselor led professional development might cover topics ranging from how faculty can support college and career readiness to the importance of understanding trauma-sensitive practices. This type of professional development helps build a community of shared understanding and also helps communicate counselors' unique roles and expertise to the entire staff while providing an important opportunity for counselors to take leadership and grow in their roles. (Plus, principals can use the money they save on bringing in outside presenters on these topics to support future professional development for the counseling department!)

As school leaders embrace their role as advocates for creating the conditions for school counselors to be effective, considering more ways to support professional development and capacity building is critical.

CULTIVATING A NEW KIND OF RELATIONSHIP

Several years ago, my husband was the principal of a large urban high school, and during that time, I saw first-hand the myriad demands placed on school leaders. Their responsibilities are endless, and they are often asked to supervise aspects of education for which they are not directly trained. However, I have also witnessed just how much a school leader can set the stage for students to have access to a strong school counseling program. In schools that I've visited where counselors are innovative and students know their counselors are there for them, I almost always hear about strong leadership that has created the conditions for that to happen. There is so much that school leaders can do in their roles—from the smallest of steps to the largest of major overhauls.

5

❖

A ROLE FOR DISTRICTS

Defining Practices That Support School-Level Change

In Denver, Colorado, Director of Counseling and College Access, Saman-tha Haviland, sees her job as "getting anything out of counselors' way that would prevent them from being successful with students." She accomplishes this by dedicating the majority of her time to communi-cating with and educating principals and other school leaders so that they can create the right conditions for the district's 125 school counsel-ors to effectively meet students' academic, social emotional, and post-secondary needs. From hiring to promoting professional development to tracking student outcomes, Haviland leads the Denver Public Schools school counseling program from her post in the Postsecondary Readiness department of the district. Across the city, school counselors and school leaders alike view Haviland as their advocate and partner. However, this culture of mutual support was not always the case.

Haviland says that for many years, school-based staff distrusted the district, seeing them only as a structure for accountability and regula-tion. Yet Haviland, herself a former school counselor, knew that counsel-ors needed much more from the district in terms of leadership. In her role, Haviland provides leadership in the form of advocacy, collaboration, cur-riculum development, grant writing, and data-driven practices. Report-ing directly to the chief of schools in the school system, Haviland attributes the shift to an array of changes including, but not limited to, induction programs for new counselors, evaluation tools for school leaders, regular meetings with other support service district leaders, and data summaries that give counselors targeted direction to their work, such as reports on students who demonstrate risk factors.

Because her hard work and leadership have earned the trust of school leaders, Haviland is routinely sought out by principals, whether they are seeking help hiring a new counselor, mentoring a struggling counselor, or finding professional development for an emerging issue in schools, such as growing rates of youth depression. Counselors, too, see her and her team of seven—whom she calls her "rock-star counselors"—as a vital source of support for the district. The team members know that counselors are being pulled in many directions and see it as their job to ensure that school leaders provide the needed leadership to help them respond to these diverse expectations. To Haviland, this systems-building work is all in service to making sure all kids in Denver receive the support they need to thrive in school and beyond.

School districts play an essential role in setting up schools and counselors for success. In many ways, districts set the tone for how school counseling can support students' academic achievement and success. Throughout this book, I have called for school counselors to use an academic home approach that provides comprehensive supports for students—a shift that depends on a clear vision and direction from the district. Without that high-level leadership, schools can encounter disconnected school initiatives, fragmentation of services, role ambiguity at the school level, notable differences in programs and services across schools, and limited innovation.

The leadership Haviland provides in the Denver Public Schools is an example of the valuable system-level support that this book calls for. A clear commitment from the school district coupled with a strong vision and system of support provides the foundation for many of the changes I describe. Despite significant changes in the field of school counseling and improvements in our understanding of how school counselors influence academic and social emotional outcomes, few school districts have yet to benefit from a systemic review and reform strategy. For school districts to invest in the kinds of leadership and programming that Haviland has enacted, they need to believe that school counseling is fundamental to achieving their mission. One counseling district leader I spoke with explained how the absence of this mindset prevents school district leaders from leveraging the potential of counselors:

> Many school districts are still reeling from naivety and neglect. In the last ten years, they've done so little with counselors. Now their task is simply to recognize what is happening to our kids. Yet, the problem is that they are so busy solving the problem of today, right now, that they can't attend to the problem of tomorrow. No thoughts about prevention. School leaders just don't have a blueprint for what counselors could be doing. And as a result, counselors aren't doing what kids need them to do.

Fortunately, however, several districts have invested in strong leadership and vision, which has created a clear blueprint for how districts can influence the work of school counselors, by aligning counselors' work across the district, providing valuable professional development, and implementing thoughtful and aligned evaluation systems. This chapter describes the role that such school districts play in supporting school-level change in school counseling. Specifically, it illustrates how establishing a district-level vision and practices that support hiring, data-driven efforts, professional development, and performance evaluations can help school districts promote more effective delivery of school counseling and support services.

STRENGTHENING DISTRICT LEADERSHIP AND ORGANIZATIONAL STRUCTURES

School districts offer important leadership to schools and counselors when they dedicate departments and staff to provide a unified vision and deploy resources to support schools' implementation of that vision. Likewise, school counselors are able to operationalize an academic home model that coordinates and monitors support services *across* academic, social emotional, and postsecondary domains when leadership at the district level plays a similar role across the district. Paying careful attention to where the school counseling department and its leadership are located within district structures is one way to achieve this goal. Because counselors' work spans multiple domains, they often need to access support and take direction from multiple departments, including departments responsible for high school support, student services, special education, college and career readiness, and community partnerships.

Where a school counseling department or office falls on a district's organization chart will ultimately shape how the work gets carried out in schools. This structural representation sends a message about how school counseling fits into the broader functioning of the district. One district I worked with many years ago demonstrated how poor placement can hamper the effectiveness of counselors. The district, which employed approximately sixty school counselors, placed a "guidance coordinator" under a department called "Ancillary Services"—a placement that sent the message, intentionally or not, that counseling was an add-on service. This orientation to school counseling as extra is not uncommon. Rather than seeing school counseling as separate from a school district's mission to educate children and prepare them for success in college and career, districts should see counselors as critical to their mission. Indeed, high-functioning school districts have moved away from situating school counseling under special education as was once the norm. Instead, successful districts have created school counseling departments that fall under a chief academic officer, a counseling and student supports department, or, in some cases, a postsecondary readiness department.

Where school counseling falls in an organizational chart also communicates clear expectations for responsibility, mechanisms for coordination and collaboration, and clear lines of authority, all of which can make a big difference in how the work gets done. A case in point:

When Nicole Cobb was the executive director of school counseling in the Metro Nashville Public Schools in Tennessee, she experienced just how important organizational structure is to district and school practices. For six of those seven years, Cobb reported to the chief academic officer, with whom she established a blueprint for how school counseling in Nashville supported students' academic achievement. When she was hired, she was charged with providing leadership to counseling programs to ensure that they were working in service to academic achievement. However, when a new superintendent restructured the district and moved school counseling under the chief of student support, this move had a significant negative impact on her work supporting counselors. According to Cobb, the biggest drawback of this move was that she "lost her seat at the table." Cobb recognized the rationale for a move, especially in light of the growing number of social emotional learning initiatives in the district and counselors' potential role in that work. At the same time, she couldn't help but notice how it simultaneously reduced her role in districtwide efforts and thus the scope of counselors' work.

Initially, situating school counseling under the academic umbrella had placed school counselors at the heart of schools. It illustrated that the work of the district's 350 school counselors was central to academic achievement. More importantly, this structure enabled Cobb to communicate a vision, create job descriptions and evaluation tools, and deliver professional services that supported the academic mission of schools. For example, when issues were raised with the leadership team about improving attendance, graduation rates, or gaps in testing, Cobb was always there to question what nonacademic barriers might be playing a role and then instruct her counseling staff to intervene as needed.

When the new superintendent restructured and moved school counseling under student support, Cobb noticed the change immediately. She was no longer invited to meetings in which curriculum and instruction were discussed and thus missed opportunities to use stu-

dents' academic data to inform counselors' work. Cobb understood that the new structure might help her and her counselors deepen their work in social emotional learning, but she couldn't help but wonder how school counselors could work effectively across multiple domains when they were pigeon-holed into one. Furthermore, she worried, shouldn't social emotional learning also be seen as part of achieving academic success?

It is difficult to say what the optimal organizational alignment for school counseling is because the answer depends to some extent on how the rest of the district is organized and other contextual factors. For example, many districts have begun to place school counseling in departments focused on college and career readiness. This decision, which is largely due to college and career falling more squarely in academic departments, positions school counselors to align their efforts with postsecondary metrics and community partners to support their students. For elementary school counselors, who align their work more with social emotional issues, however, this placement may not work best. Even for high school counselors, this structure has the potential to disconnect their work from other important aspects of their position.

Where counseling falls in the organizational chart also determines the authority and supervision chain. In most school districts, school counselors report directly to their principals. However, they may also take direction from a district leader, as is true for the counselors in Denver and Nashville. In some cases, when school counselors' work falls under the purview of multiple departments (e.g., academic, special education, career and technical education), counselors can find themselves responsible to multiple supervisors. This situation can be remedied by clear coordination at the district level, but this is not always the case. Confusion about roles and direction is common, as Cobb found:

Shortly after hosting professional development with her counselors on the topic of the ASCA Model, including the social emotional standards that are included in the ASCA National Standards, Cobb received a call from one of her middle school counselors. The principal had told this counselor that the director of the Social Emotional Learning (SEL) department had created a curriculum and the school leader expected the counselors in the school to implement it in classrooms. Unclear about how this curriculum fit with the counseling curriculum created by Cobb's office, the counselor was confused. She wondered if she was supposed to follow the directive of the school counseling office or the SEL department.

The lack of alignment between the two departments in the same district is not only frustrating but also wasteful. Instead, Cobb says, the two departments might have found a way to crosswalk the two sets of standards to create one coherent set along with accompanying curriculum and resources. This kind of coordination is more likely when district leadership is centrally located and committed to helping schools connect services and communicate across programs, initiatives, and departments. Without such collaboration, districts risk fragmented services, lack of data sharing, frustration with partners, and even missed opportunities to share resources, such as professional development.

SETTING A VISION

This alignment and collaboration are easier when each department and staff member working in the district is guided by a clear vision. For schools to establish school counseling programs and missions, school districts should develop a vision for how school counseling can work in service to the district's goals. A clear vision for school counseling includes many things. To begin with, mission statements can articulate what a district hopes students will be able to do because of their school counseling program. This framing, which is endorsed by ASCA, puts the focus on outcomes and identifies school counseling as promoting skills and development that set up students for success in school and life. Districts are then positioned to enact that vision through job descriptions, templates and tools, and professional development. Also, school counselors and counseling departments can use that vision to set yearly goals and track data to determine whether they reach those goals. Some districts even articulate how much time counselors should dedicate to different aspects of their programming to meet the district's expectations of counselors.

Creating a vision also means articulating the kinds of supports to which all students will have access, regardless of which school they attend. By articulating what resources a district hopes to provide for students, district leaders can better guide school leaders about how to support their counselors' time. In the absence of a clear vision, school leaders struggle to figure out how to incorporate school counseling into their schools. An urban high school principal I interviewed several years ago described a missed opportunity to prepare a group of incoming school leaders with a districtwide vision for school counseling:

> There's a week-long orientation, and I came in with, like, thirty other new leaders; there are a lot of new leaders. . . . There was not one mention of support resources, mental health, and this is one of the biggest problems here! They paraded before us people from facilities, a lot of instructional pieces, which is good, but no one to say, "This is going to be a significant part of your work." I'm feeling like that leaves people like me on my own, trying to figure out what would be a feasible, substantive, well-working system. I have to figure that out on my own.

Although this principal and others like him might be inclined to hold high expectations for school counselors, a lack of direction from the district can make delivering on that difficult. In an ideal world, appointed school leaders already understand how school counseling fits into a school; however, the reality is that some enter into this role needing some education from practicing counselors.

Several years ago, I received a request from a school superintendent who was looking to hire a new director of guidance and counseling and wondered if I had anyone to recommend. I began by asking the superintendent what he wanted from this new director (e.g., skills and expertise). When the superintendent finished detailing the functions of the former director that mostly included test management, special education management, and master scheduling, I said that I was sorry; I could not help him. I then explained that if he were open to a different model and hiring a dynamic district leader who could create a school counseling vision that incorporated data, leveraged partners, and built on national best practices to drive student achievement, I'd be happy to send him some names. Like many district leaders, this superintendent did not even know such a role was possible. However, our conversation led to his revamping the position and hiring someone who orchestrated major changes in the district.

The good news is that updating an outdated vision is doable. Chances are there are many counselors who would readily welcome the opportunity to reenvision their roles and inform a districtwide vision. This way, counselors can bring their understanding of the field and best practices to a new vision. Importantly, engaging counselors in a planning process can ensure that a new vision is aligned with a set of principles and practices that guide the work.

CREATING AND ENABLING DATA-DRIVEN SYSTEMS

An essential principle that informs the vision of many district school counseling programs is the use of data-driven practices. Although many outside the school counseling profession may not be aware of this, data-driven decision-making is a cornerstone of the ASCA National Model, and as a result, many school counselors around the country regularly use data to demonstrate program success, identify student needs, uncover disparities in access to opportunities, and understand pressing issues in the school context.[1] Likewise, many counselor educators have covered this topic in depth, contributing to a trend in evidence-based school counseling.[2] Although this movement has gained decent traction in the school counseling community, many counselors are still not on board, and importantly, only a few districts provide the infrastructure for successful use of data. A national survey of counselors conducted by the College Board's National Office for School Counselor Advocacy (NOSCA) found that only 59 percent of high school counselors and 57 percent of those from middle schools know how to use data to conduct needs assessments for individual students.[3] Studies show that many school counselors are interested in using data in their work; however, low levels of confidence, time constraints, limited access to data systems, and school leaders who do not value evidence-based practices continue to stand in their way.[4]

Because data-driven practices can play a big role in implementing an academic home approach to school counseling, district support for them is critical. In some of the strongest districts I've visited, school counselors use data to target specific interventions and supports. In these cases, districts (or sometimes third-party vendors) create and send data reports and summaries that direct counselors' efforts. The District of Columbia Public Schools (DCPS) system offers a great example of this:

Several years ago, DCPS officials began to wonder about how its students were faring in college. Unable to locate any specific in-house data on these postsecondary outcomes, they turned to the National Student Clearinghouse, which publishes postsecondary enrollment, mobility, and degree attainment rates for students who graduated from a given school or district. The staff in the DCPS Office of College and Career Education knew this was data that principals had not seen before and immediately started sharing the data in individual meetings. At that time, school leaders were focused on graduation rates and not giving much thought to students' post-high school outcomes. However, things changed very quickly. How the district moved from 59 percent of the class of 2015 applying to at least one college to 80 percent four years later is a story about data and how collaborative efforts between the district, schools, and community partners can make a difference.

Led by Kimberly Hanauer and Erin Bibo-Ward, the Office of College and Career Education began to show school leaders postsecondary data that were compelling and easily understood, and that illustrated clear gaps in programing. They then asked principals to set clear postsecondary goals, something the principals had not been asked to do before. To keep schools on track and give them clear guidance about where to target their efforts, Hanauer and her team sent out a monthly "College Data Roundup." This mash-up of data, which drew from national and district sources, showcased progress of each student toward meeting districtwide postsecondary goals. These reports illustrated trends based on existing data already available to them, such as PSAT, FAFSA, application data, and even EFC (Expected Family Contribution) information. Recently, this office added four metrics for career education to balance out career preparation with college and career readiness. For instance, a school leader and counselor can now track how many students completed a resume or participated in a mock interview. Importantly, they can see whether gaps exist between who is and is not on track to meet schoolwide goals and intervene accordingly.

According to Hanauer, giving schools this postsecondary data allowed the district to have informed conversations with school leaders and identify possible interventions to help meet their schoolwide goals. Over the four-year span during which this data-driven practice was implemented, the district saw increases in SAT participation, FAFSA completion, and college applications and acceptances. And, importantly, the schools have become adept at letting data guide their work.

To ensure that schools can deliver comprehensive student supports, they need access to robust data systems; they also need to receive (or create themselves) data summaries to guide their work. When schools have access to such systems, they are in a better position to set yearly goals for individual students and the school as a whole. With baseline data already available, school counselors can also work with network partners to set yearly goals based on gaps in current outcomes. Counselors can even engage students in looking at schoolwide data and gathering their insight into what improvements are needed.

Data-driven practices make it possible for school counselors to enact an academic home vision by providing concrete evidence about trends in student experience or challenges. For example, the intervention team at TechBoston Academy, described previously, saw a pattern in student cases that revealed behaviors associated with trauma. This observation led the school to dedicate schoolwide professional development time to trauma-sensitive practices. One could also imagine examining referrals traditionally sent to an intervention team to ask other valuable questions, such as which teachers refer the most students to counseling, what are the most common interventions used by teachers, or whether there are course-taking patterns among particular student groups.

With these types of data, school counselors and their network partners can also track students' affiliation with enrichment and extracurricular opportunities and subsequently identify ways to expand opportunities to reach students who are otherwise disconnected. For example, when counselors use teams to work collaboratively with postsecondary planning partners, they might look at who is and who is not being well served by external partners and make a plan to remedy any gaps in opportunity and participation.

District leaders do not have to lead this effort alone or create resources from scratch. The expectation that school counselors use data is reinforced by many resources, books, trainings, and tools. For example, counselor educator and former school counselor Trish Hatch operates a nonprofit called Hatching Results, which provides education, training, and consultation for schools and counselors looking to expand their data-driven work. Likewise, the Evidence-Based School Counseling Conference, which was started many years ago to increase counselors' efficacy with using data, runs an annual conference attended by many school counselors who wish to learn more about data-driven counseling.

The work of Cheryl Holcomb-McCoy concerning the role school counselors play in closing the achievement gap includes numerous examples of how school counselors use a data-driven approach to identify patterns that limit opportunity for marginalized students.[5]

One reason behind DCPS's success is its focus on providing postsecondary data reports to school leaders rather than only to counselors and their college access partners. This strategy, which came from meetings with school leaders illustrating how little they had focused on these outcomes, ultimately positioned counselors to engage in their work.

Looking back on their success with creating a data-driven culture in the postsecondary domain, Hanauer notes that a breakthrough occurred when her team realized that getting this information directly to school leaders was key. From meetings with school leaders, Hanauer and her colleagues learned that school principals didn't know they could be benchmarking their effectiveness based on the postsecondary experiences of their students. Hanauer and her team realized that a lot of the strategies they had been using were directed straight to the school counseling staff. In Hanauer's mind, "school staff care about what the school leader cares about." So, they got the school leaders to care by showing them data they otherwise did not have access to.

To assure that counselors are using data to drive their programming, school districts like DCPS play an important supporting role. According to Chrys Dougherty, a senior scientist from the ACT who writes extensively on student information systems, districts can promote the use of data in many ways to improve student outcomes in schools. Among the strategies that Dougherty calls for, a few speak specifically to school counseling.[6] These strategies include developing and refining behavioral goals, identifying what information counselors and other educators need to know, creating data platforms that are accessible to school leaders and link various data sets, producing timely and user-friendly reports, making knowledge of and experience with using data a hiring criterion, and embedding data-driven practices into professional development plans.[7]

Although districts may not have the capability to overhaul their data infrastructures completely, they can implement training programs to increase the data fluency of counselors. Fairfax County Public Schools in Northern Virginia is one district that implemented a comprehensive data training program for the district's 255 elementary school counselors. The initiative included four half-day training programs ("Data Mondays") that focused on how to develop action plans, as well as how to collect, analyze, and share data.[8] In this way, districts can also provide important leadership by teaching others how to create their own summary reports.

HIRING AND SUPPORTING NEW COUNSELORS

The districtwide strategies I have described will be most successful if schools are able to hire highly qualified school counselors. This hiring process, which includes everything from creating a job description, recruiting strong candidates, assessing their goodness of fit for a particular school or district, and interviewing, can be difficult for school leaders with little training in this area. The growth of site-based control has left many school leaders responsible for hiring school counselors and onboarding them for work in their buildings. While districts differ in terms of how they handle hiring, districts with strong counseling leadership provide school leaders support for hiring. In some districts this means providing principals sample interview questions, reviewing and screening resumes of potential employees, or even joining an interview team. In addition, school districts that have dedicated school counseling offices can also play a part in aligning job descriptions with the district vision at-large and its school counseling vision in particular, providing support for screening and hiring, and coordinating early orientation and mentoring options.

Hiring is just the first step. New hires also require essential support for onboarding and early career mentoring.

In Denver, Samantha Haviland spends a week with new counselor hires, during which time she provides an overview of what is expected of counselors and the kinds of resources that are available for them to use in their work. Perhaps the most important aspect of this induction process is the relationship building that occurs. Creating these lasting relationships and trust sets an important foundation for future mentorship and feedback over the course of their career in Denver Public Schools. This onboarding process does not end there. During the year Haviland spends forty-five hours with new counselors reviewing district policies, ASCA implementation, and best practices used by the district and also building a trusting relationship. Haviland knows, however, that she is not the only source of support for new counselors. Therefore, she utilizes the expertise of all her counselors through email and online discussion spaces that allow counselors to share resources and provide support for one another.

This rich induction experience sends an important message to counselors that they will be supported in their roles. Some big districts are beginning to host monthly meetings for new counselors to support their transition and onboarding. In other districts, new counselors are offered mentoring programs to help introduce professionals to the field. These programs, which have traditionally been more common for teachers, pair counselors in their first three years with more experienced counselors to provide support on the job, resource sharing, information about the district, and professional guidance. Although such mentoring programs are not the norm, they should be. Instead, school counselors are often required to attend teacher orientations, which have limited relevance to their jobs, and find themselves seeking mentorship on their own, if at all. Fortunately, some states are helping districts create better opportunities for counselors. For example, the North Carolina School Counseling Association matches counselors in their first three years of the job with an experienced counselor and encourages them to connect in person, in groups, or virtually throughout the year.

CREATING MEANINGFUL PROFESSIONAL LEARNING AND DEVELOPMENT

If districts are going to put school counselors in the position to lead in an academic home framework, they also need to provide them the professional learning opportunities to refine their practice and learn new skills. Having these opportunities is especially important because graduate school curricula may not be aligned with what is now expected of counselors. Many programs favor clinical counseling courses with little attention to the leadership, advocacy, and data-driven practices that are crucial skills in enacting the academic home vision for the role of a counselor. Even if changes in higher education take hold, districts should support the counselors who have already completed graduate study and thus missed the chance for preservice training in these areas. Even when graduate programs have offered such training, professional learning is critical to counselors' work because of changing social contexts and the need to bring real-world problems of practice to the learning of content. School leaders play an important role in ensuring their counselors are able to participate in professional development. If districts provide meaningful professional development that is aligned with schoolwide goals and a counseling vision, school leaders are more likely to support counselors' attendance.

Professional development and learning content must be driven by the needs of students, counselors, and schools. This often means differentiating the content based on the roles counselors are playing and key issues relevant to their particular school or district. Differing developmental needs, varying staffing structures, and varying levels of parental engagement all contribute to counselors performing slightly different roles. For example, elementary school counselors spend a lot of their time promoting children's social skills, school adjustment, and decision-making, as well as providing consultation to teachers and family members. This work requires professional development that enhances counselors' content knowledge and skills working with younger populations. On the other hand, because high school students have different schedules and move around the school more than younger students, group and classroom counseling methods are less common in high schools. Some studies report that high school counselors currently spend the majority of their time on academic and postsecondary development, with less time dedicated to social emotional development.[9] As you can imagine, their needs as professionals will vary given this wide range of contexts. Nonetheless, some skills are applicable across developmental domains for all counselors, such as how to use data to inform practice, that can be the subject of common professional development.

The job of district leaders who provide professional development to counselors is to organize it in a way that is accessible and desirable. Counselors are sometimes reluctant to attend professional development due to demanding schedules and administrators' lack of support. However, in Granite School District in Utah, nearly 100 percent of counselors attend district-sponsored professional development.

Granite State School District's Director of College and Career Readiness, Judy Petersen, knows just how difficult it is to justify leaving the building to attend professional development. Yet, as a former school counselor, she also recognizes just how valuable it can be to attend high-quality professional learning. With this in mind, she provides monthly professional development to the district's one hundred counselors but lets them choose between a morning or afternoon session. Peterson believes that offering counselors this choice and allowing them to remain in their schools for half of the day contributes to their high attendance rate.

Petersen also knows that counselors' partnership with principals is a core aspect of their work and integrates this philosophy into her pro-

fessional learning programs. Annually, the district hosts the Annual Counselor Institute, where counselors and principals review yearly agreements, goals, and expectations for the year. This event, which typically achieves 100 percent attendance, and the others hosted by the district reflect the district's philosophy that professional learning "is an expectation of your work."

In places that promote a culture of valued professional learning, school district leaders routinely survey counselors for content and structures that will best meet their professional needs. Some districts, such as Granite School District, maintain a steering committee that is composed of one school counselor from each school and charged with advising the district on many things, including professional development plans.

Many school districts are experimenting with professional learning communities (PLC) as a way to support the professional growth of educators. A PLC has been described as a group of educators collaboratively engaging in collective inquiry and action research to better support the students they serve.[10] PLCs typically identify a problem of practice, test strategies to address that problem, and reflect together to make ongoing improvements. Within the school counseling profession, PLCs can be arranged by school, grade level, or specialty area. PLCs may include other related school personnel such as social workers, nurses, or college advisors. Strategically including educators such as special education personnel fosters increased collaboration between professionals in these two distinct areas.[11] PLCs can also be organized by geographic area; this type of model can be great for counselors who work in isolation, such as those in small or rural districts. School districts can support PLCs by bringing counselors together over shared interests.

In the Cherokee County School District in Georgia, Supervisor of Student Services, Rouel Belleza, created his own type of PLC: counselor learning groups (CLG). Belleza wanted to create professional learning opportunities that responded to the diverse needs of the eighty-five counselors in the district, while also building community across schools and grade levels.

Based on a survey that highlighted counselors' interest in such topics as mental health, K–5 curriculum, at-risk populations, and LGBTQ issues, Belleza created monthly CLGs and invited counselors across the district to join a group for the year. Belleza used a staggered, rotating schedule to convene these groups once a month for approximately two-and-a-half hours. With this time, each CLG meets in a shared space provided at one of the schools to discuss topics of interest to them and their work. Belleza sees his role as "creating the space, facilitating, and offering guidance, not answers." He accomplishes this by sharing examples from other districts, structuring their time effectively, and offering parameters when needed.

As one example, many elementary counselors were interested in a K–5 developmental counseling curriculum. After reviewing other models and content about children's social emotional needs, this CLG created lessons on topics such as friendship, relationships, problem solving, and identity development that could be shared and utilized across the district.

Belleza believes that this approach to professional learning provides an opportunity for professionals "who feel strongly about a particular topic to connect with colleagues to focus on what needs to happen for the district to better understand the topic, gather best practices to address an issue, and how to implement changes in their schools." Describing these CLGs as truly collegial and much better than traditional professional development, Belleza sees this approach to professional learning as especially useful at bringing together counselors across schools and grade levels who are learning together about shared interests.

This example highlights what is possible when district leaders with a focus on school counseling tailor a professional learning practice, traditionally used with teachers, to meet school counselors' unique needs.

Another less common but important kind of professional development for school counselors is self-care. Certainly, everyone working in schools can benefit from self-care, but this is particularly true for school counselors who spend the majority of their time helping struggling students and, in some cases, internalizing the stressors that their students face. A few years ago, I asked groups of urban school counselors what they needed from their district leaders. Out of six focus groups, five of them involved a good deal of tears. Some counselors cried about their frustration at not being able to do their jobs as well as they desired; others were stressed to a level they found difficult to manage, like this counselor:

> This year, there was a major crisis in the school: a student died. It was awful. Yet, we didn't have anyone from district reach out—no one asked how they can help. The principal did and my supervisor did, but no one from higher up. We lack that kind of leadership.

In each school represented in these focus groups, some type of tragedy had occurred in the school or broader community. Sadly, this is not unusual, and not limited to urban schools. We often take for granted the support counselors provide to others in these times; it is common practice for principals to send an email or letter stating that school counselors are always "on hand" to provide students extra support or resources. It can be easy to forget that counselors need support, too. Without that, counselors are at high risk for burnout. School counseling has one of the highest turnover rates of any profession, with 60 percent of counselors leaving the field within two years.[12] This turnover can be linked to high stress levels associated with managing taxing caseloads, overseeing multiple job responsibilities, and receiving limited clinical supervision, as well as constant exposure to student stress and trauma.[13] Burnout detrimentally impacts not only counselors but also the students they serve. Research has found that burnout can negatively impact the services that counselors provide and the amount of time counselors work directly with their students.[14] Of course, burnout also consumes resources and threatens efficiency, especially when burnout leads to turnover and new counselors must be hired and trained.

Using professional development time to facilitate self-care means reminding staff to take care of themselves and also providing dedicated time and structures to allow counseling staff to process the stress they are experiencing and find outlets for managing it. This may mean encouraging staff to get enough sleep, turning off technology, or learning to recognize the signs of burnout, or it can take the form of peer support or mindfulness sessions designed to meet counselors' individual and personal needs. School counselors may also be uniquely qualified to provide professional development for teachers and workshops for students about self-care, thereby reinforcing these crucial messages for themselves.

COLLABORATING ON PERFORMANCE EVALUATIONS

When districts hold high expectations for counselors, give them useful tools to aid their work, support their transition into the role, and provide high-quality professional learning, school counselors will be poised to be held accountable for their work. Performance evaluations are most commonly used to measure success and ensure effectiveness. For all professionals, performance evaluations are essential mechanisms to support growth and improvement. If developed and used appropriately, these evaluations can be a powerful tool to create alignment between school-wide goals and school counseling work. Particularly in schools that have a strong feedback culture, in which professionals feel safe and encouraged to ask for feedback, the evaluation process can be seen as a supportive endeavor, especially when paired with observations by trained professionals.

Whereas schools once lacked the tools to carry out counselor evaluations, this is no longer the case. Between state tools, ASCA templates, and district-created evaluation instruments, districts have numerous options to use for counselor evaluations. The availability of such options is a big improvement from a time when counselors were evaluated using teacher tools and based on teaching criteria. These updated tools reflect a comprehensive school counseling model and are based on the professional standards of practice developed for school counselors including attention to direct services to students and systems management and coordination. Statewide evaluations provide useful tools for districts to use, complete with observation resources.

An important factor in evaluating school counselors is who does the evaluating. When school counselors are evaluated by school leaders who have little understanding of their role, counselors miss an opportunity for constructive feedback that can help them improve. For this reason, many school districts have utilized a collaborative approach that pairs a district counseling leader with a school leader to conduct the evaluation. Ideally, this process incorporates observations so that counselors have an opportunity to receive observational feedback.

For too long, education leaders assumed there was no way to observe counselors, due to the confidential nature of their work. However, things have changed. In fact, in many states and districts, counselor observations are required and part of the overall evaluation process. School and district leaders might consider observing counselors leading classroom lessons, team meetings that include network partners, and conversations with students about academic plans and other discussions that are unlikely to include a lot of personal information.

As one district leader learned, a collaborative evaluation process can increase school leaders' understanding of counseling and ability to conduct future evaluations. In Nashville, both district- and school-level administrators conduct supervision and evaluation, and that process has been educational for school leaders.

Tennessee state policy requires that school counselors have multiple observations throughout the year, followed by postconference meetings. The exact number of observations depends on a counselor's years of experience, with new counselors required to have four observations during the year. In many districts, school leaders assume responsibility for completing all of these observations in a given year for all counselors—no small feat. However, to lighten their load, Nicole Cobb partnered with school principals, splitting the number of observations and building relationships in the process. This practice, although difficult in the beginning, ultimately built school leaders' capacity to provide better supervision for their counselors.

Although the person who conducted the observation normally carried out the postconference, Cobb participated in the majority of these discussions, even those for which she did not complete the observation. Cobb knew that doing these conferences together with the school principal would be an important step toward forming a collaborative relationship and building trust; however, it also helped school leaders, who initially struggled to give feedback on practices with which they were unfamiliar.

After each observation, Cobb emailed the principal to request availability for the postconference and then used Google Hangouts or Skype to bring in participants. Surprisingly, no one ever said no to her! These virtual meetings became the norm, except in cases when a school counselor was struggling and required more critical feedback. In those cases, a more formal in-person meeting took place.

Over the course of the year, Cobb completed between 100 and 150 observations and nearly 350 postconference sessions. She managed to keep these meetings to thirty minutes by sending clear instructions to counselors about how to prepare. Although completing all these observations was still a heavy lift for her, Cobb knew it had to happen. She had previously reviewed counselor evaluations and saw how subjective they were. She read positive evaluations of counselors who were doing few counselor-specific functions. Although she knew her peers in other districts would leave this task to school administrators to carry out, Cobb felt strongly that these observations be completed by someone who had been in counselors' shoes at one time.

Cobb knew that expecting school leaders to attend the postconference meetings was a big ask. Initially, Cobb believed that sharing this responsibility ensured that she and the principal were on the same page. However, it didn't take long before principals saw their value. They often asked if they could video these meetings so that they could watch Cobb later. Principals praised her approach with counselors and expressed wanting to use some of the same questions with teachers. Perhaps most notably, these meetings helped Cobb build positive relationships with these school leaders.

Many states have adopted school counseling standards that are used to guide programmatic efforts. These standards-based frameworks are also used to guide evaluations of school counselors. When districts adopt statewide frameworks and ensure that school counselors' responsibilities, expectations, professional development, and professional resources align with these standards, statewide evaluation tools and protocols can be extremely valuable. In the absence of these state policies, districts can and should adopt appropriate evaluation tools that accurately capture the scope of counselors' day-to-day practices.

SETTING UP SCHOOLS AND STUDENTS FOR SUCCESS

After several years as the executive director of school counseling, Nicole Cobb began hearing from counselors that they were spending too much time as testing coordinators in their schools. She knew this to be a longstanding problem in other districts and that schools often relied heavily on school counselors to assist with testing. Until now, Cobb rationalized that the counselors just had to get through the heavy testing month; however, the uptick in complaints made her wonder if something had changed. Using a needs assessment to evaluate how the school counselors were spending their time, Cobb intended to use data to advocate for limitations on counselors' test-

ing duties. Instead, Cobb found that she woefully underestimated the situation.

As she read through the open-ended responses to her survey, Cobb learned that the school counselors were in charge of far more testing than she realized. In addition to the yearly statewide assessments in the spring, her counselors were also in charge of various other assessments. Counselors reported that they were coordinating and proctoring nearly monthly assessments. On average, her counselors were spending approximately one week out of every month with testing. As a result, counselors' time with students was heavily compromised.

Cobb decided it was time for a change and believed her strong relationship with the superintendent provided the right setup. In a presentation to the superintendent, she described her understanding of the district priorities, including reducing chronic absenteeism, limiting discipline disparities, and closing gaps in achievement by race, which she knew well given her position under the chief academic officer. She then explained how her counselors were currently spending their time (presenting data from her assessment), followed by a description of the kinds of things counselors could be doing instead, such as conducting home visits, delivering curriculum in grade nine classes, and leading groups with disengaged students. She explained, "We have curriculum sitting on the shelves, interventions not being implemented. Here is what they could be doing."

The superintendent had no idea. He was disappointed to learn that counselors were spending so much time on testing and, as a result, not carrying out the programming the district believed would help tackle its most pressing issues.

She closed her presentation by sharing how much the district was paying counselors and questioned, "Is this what we want them doing?" Instead, Cobb recommended hiring retired teachers to assist with testing and asking other school partners to assist with test proctoring and management. Together they hatched a new plan. Counsel-

ors would continue to support testing by identifying students, making spreadsheets with student needs and accommodations, and talking with students about text anxiety. However, they would no longer be in charge of all of it. Eventually, the superintendent took things one step further. He gave schools a directive: schools can no longer name counselors testing coordinators, and all counselors must spend about 80 percent of their time on student-facing work.

District counseling leaders like Nicole Cobb and Samantha Haviland are leading the system-level efforts that are necessary for school counselors to effectively create and deliver academic homes for students. Without question, district leaders can have a big impact on whether school counselors are able to implement the kinds of programs, interventions, and practices that have been shown to lead to improved outcomes, and they are therefore a worthwhile staffing investment for districts to make. However, superintendents and other district leaders play a big part in how these district visions are carried out. In places where superintendents have committed financial and human capital to support school counseling, thus positioning their counselors to be effective, students have benefitted.

6

✜

PHILANTHROPY AND POLICY

Building Capacity for School Counseling Reform

When the newly appointed superintendent of the Boston Public Schools named arts education as one of her top priorities, many people were cautiously optimistic. Residents of the city knew that the new superintendent had successfully used the arts to improve education in her previous appointment in Memphis, and they also knew that Boston had a rich arts community that could help make her goal a reality.

At the same time, arts education had not recently played a big role in the schools. Less than 10 percent of the city's elementary and middle school children were receiving arts education twice a week, the standard best practice.[1] Only about a quarter of the city's high schools offered arts instruction to more than 25 percent of their students.[2] Although terrific youth and community programs were offering arts opportunities to Boston's children, these programs were fragmented and their reach was limited. Even more troubling, the uneven availability of arts programming meant a child's access to arts education was predetermined by where that child attended school. Laura Perille, then executive director of EdVestors, a school improvement organization that utilizes private investments to support the Boston Public Schools, knew that helping the superintendent make good on her arts priority was going to require major systemic change. This is precisely what she and her colleagues helped to do over the next nine years.

With vision, strategy, and a collective-action approach, EdVes-
tors successfully created a public/private partnership that generated
shared interest in and responsibility for arts education; today this ini-
tiative is known as the Boston Public Schools Arts Expansion (BPS-
AE). What started out as a goal to widen access to the arts in schools
ultimately became a citywide movement that brought educators, local
philanthropists, community partners, business leaders, parents, and
youth together to advance arts education in the city of Boston. With
support from all of these stakeholders and working together with the
school's administration, EdVestors expanded access to arts opportu-
nities for students while also improving arts curriculum, instruction,
and professional development. This initiative also enhanced assess-
ments, partnership coordination, communication, and ongoing data
reviews to measure progress. In short, this initiative made quality arts
education the norm in the city of Boston.

The Boston Public Schools Arts Expansion initiative is an example of
the kind of systemic change that is needed to bring the school counseling vision described in this book to reality. Like the arts, school counselors' work is supported by an array of community-based programs,
higher education partners, and out-of-school programs that share an
interest in students' academic, social emotional, and postsecondary success. However, fragmentation and a lack of aligned systems undermine
real possibility for change. Like arts programming, many schools and districts need stronger infrastructure and supports in place to improve the
quality of school counseling. The changes that I call for in this book will
require stakeholders throughout the field of education to think and act
differently, as happened with the arts stakeholders in Boston. Similar to
arts education in many districts, school counseling has not yet been seen
as a priority, and the kind of system change that increased access to high-
quality arts education and leveraged community arts groups in Boston is
necessary if we want to put counselors at the center of student support.
School counselors, school and district leaders, and other educators will

need to reframe what they think school counseling can do to bring about positive change in schools across academic, social emotional, and post-secondary domains.

The powerful work of EdVestors and its partners prove not only that this kind of change is possible but also that school counselors and their school and district leaders can't do it alone. Their success depends on those who work in philanthropy and policy to join them in the effort to bring forth a new vision. Philanthropists and policy makers, committed to students' development and achievement, need a shared understanding of the impact school counseling reform can have on students and of the importance of a system and supports that enable them to be effective.

In this chapter, I describe how private philanthropy, as well as state and federal governments, can refocus their energies and support school counseling reform in schools and districts. Specifically, I describe the important role that private philanthropy can play in building district and school capacity to establish and manage an academic home model. I illustrate how investments in large-scale school counseling reform have the potential to advance development in multiple outcome areas instead of focusing on one particular set of outcomes. This chapter also recommends changes in policy, such as mandated school counseling programs and ratios, licensure requirements, and data availability, that support the recommendations made in previous chapters. Throughout this chapter, I highlight examples of organizations and states that are leading the way.

PHILANTHROPY

For educators to create the kind of change that is necessary to broadly enact an academic home framework, they will need new resources. In the words of Carol Johnson, former Boston and Memphis superintendent who initiated the expansion of arts in Boston, "Schools get money to provide instruction and are expected to do the rest for free."[3] As a result, much of the financial support that schools use to support academic enrichment, college and career readiness, and social emotional learning and health has come from private foundations. Critics of education funders have questioned whether private philanthropy overly influences educational practices.[4] Indeed, when a private donor makes funding available in a way that is not driven or informed by educators, there is a risk of undue influence. On the other hand, external pressures can hold bureaucratic systems accountable for best practices and outcomes that they might otherwise neglect.

Private philanthropy plays a much bigger role in education today than it has in the past. According to Sarah Reckhow, an educational researcher who writes extensively on how philanthropy has changed school practices and policies, private giving to education exploded in the 2000s with the entrance of the Bill and Melinda Gates Foundation and other large foundations.[5] This is certainly true of social emotional health and postsecondary readiness, both of which have been targets of private philanthropy over the past several years. According to *Inside Philanthropy*, college readiness has emerged "as one of the leading education reform efforts of the 21st century."[6] A report by the Institute for Higher Education Policy found that about 68 percent of the Fortune 100 companies examined in their study support college- and career-readiness opportunities through their philanthropic efforts.[7] Big foundations such as the Gates Foundation and smaller foundations such as the Kresge Foundation and Michael and Susan Dell Foundation list nonprofit college access programs as recipients. Likewise, foundation support represents a significant source of private funding for school mental health and social emotional development programs.[8] These organizations provide funds that support both the provision of mental health promotion and prevention-related programming.[9]

Despite major investments in these areas, private philanthropy has largely veered away from investments that create the kind of structural changes to schools seen in the case of EdVestors and the BPS-AE. Instead, foundations and donors have focused on investments in nonprofit organizations and charter schools.[10] These investments in resources and efforts external to public schools often spring from a troubling deficit-focused perspective about schools that tries to compensate for structural problems in schools rather than addressing them. For example, many foundations with an interest in postsecondary degree attainment direct funding to nonprofit organizations that either "push in" to schools to deliver services or operate in communities. Specifically, this strategy has been used to equalize opportunity for students by giving them access to resources that evidence suggests are essential to educational achievement or opportunity but may otherwise be missing in schools.

Investing in the Hub, Not Just the Spokes

The approach needs to change. The current overemphasis on investing in programs aimed to fill the gaps in the system is like creating a wheel with lots of spokes without also establishing the hub. Without attention to the hub, the spokes can't work as well. Applying this analogy to school-based student supports, investing resources in the spokes can mean not serving all students, duplicating services, or missing the importance of coordination across efforts. Certainly, private investment in nonprofit and community programs is sorely needed. With limited subsidies from state governments, nonprofit organizations rely heavily on private dollars to support their existence. However, this investment does not need to, and should not, come at the exclusion of support for public schools. For school counselors to provide all students an academic home that responds to and promotes their academic, social emotional, and postsecondary development, financial resources that have typically gone *to augment* the system need to be directed *to help* the system. That is, funders will need to see school counselors and academic homes as central to their interests and redirect investments in a way that enables school counselors to lead a coordinated system of supports across all three domains of their work.

On the other hand, when community-based programs work in partnership with school-based efforts, and a strong foundation is in place in schools to coordinate and strengthen the many partners, everyone benefits, especially students. Such benefits can be seen in the Boston arts example.

> When EdVestors took on the arts expansion work, the organization realized that the current model of providing external funding to innovative projects and supporting alternative arts education was not being scaled. As a result, some students were getting enriching arts opportunities while others were not so fortunate. EdVestors discovered that one reason for this piecemeal and inequitable pattern was the lack of an internal district system to equitably invest external dollars and resources. Its leaders quickly realized that, with educational leadership invested in arts education, hundreds of arts and cultural organizations ready to engage, and its own strong reputation as an organization with a track record in helping schools improve, the time was right to confront the systemic challenges.
>
> EdVestors' main task became creating a strong internal system that could effectively make use of many valuable community and higher education partners. A primary goal of this initiative was improved coordination of partnerships with arts and cultural groups and higher education. To achieve this, EdVestors created an Arts Expansion Fund to provide grant funds to support expanded arts programming in schools, established a database of arts offerings in the city, provided a small stipend for school-based staff members already working in Boston Public Schools to serve as an arts liaison and to be the point of contact for all arts activities, and added a central office position— an executive director for the arts. These positions were based in the school system and initially funded by EdVestors but eventually taken over by the school district.
>
> According to Marinell Rousmaniere, a key leader of BPS-AE at EdVestors, providing a short-term investment for staffing was critical to support the initial district capacity. Though not intended to be permanent, giving a small stipend to the arts liaisons enabled that

person to bring people together, put systems in place, and play a leadership role in the arts at their school. Using staff already working in the school provided an important signal that their time was valued and that building internal capacity was critical to the success of the initiative. Though the stipends have typically not continued beyond the initial startup period, arts liaisons continue to play this role in schools today.

In addition to increasing support, a benefit of philanthropic investments in the "hub" is that they can serve as a conduit to leverage increased public investments among schools and districts, in the manner that the BPS-AE did. By providing initial funds for the district to hire a strong arts leader who could lead this transformation internally and support school leaders whose expertise was not in the arts, the BPS-AE created the appetite for the district to eventually assume this cost.

Like schools, the district also needed leadership and capacity building. In this regard, EdVestors supported the hiring of a senior arts leader as executive director for the arts at Boston Public Schools. Myran Parker-Brass, a highly influential arts leader, was drawn to the position because of the districts' elevation of the arts. The accomplished singer and administrator was influential in helping the district and schools make good decisions about arts education. Because Parker-Brass knew what good arts education looked like, she helped principals hire talented arts educators, evaluate and provide professional support to struggling staff, and improve arts instruction across the city. Ultimately, the success that Parker-Brass brought to the district compelled them to continue to invest in this role.

As was true for the BPS-AE, the school district found that when strong district infrastructure and leadership provided technical assistance and guidance to schools, access to the arts increased and existing arts education improved. Investments in school counseling that work to change the core vision and practices at the district level can have a similar impact on school-based counseling programs and supports. In fact, funders who already support school enrichment programs such as college access or youth development might find that their existing investments could be more influential, and thus their equity goals realized, if they simultaneously invested in the core of educational practice.

Supporting Large-scale Change

Private foundations also play a key role in piloting reforms that have the potential to influence large-scale change. For example, some private investments resemble the EdVestors approach to arts education but on a larger scale (i.e., states or regions). This is the approach the Lilly Endowment has taken to address with statewide challenges concerning students' postsecondary degree attainment and overall mental health.

In 2016, the Lilly Endowment launched a five-year grant, the Comprehensive Counseling Initiative, to strengthen the quality of K–12 school counseling programs in Indiana schools. This investment was motivated by research highlighting the inadequacy of Indiana school counseling programs in meeting the academic, behavioral, and social emotional needs of all students in the state. Because the foundation is committed to education within Indiana, it was moved to invest in school counseling after reviewing data showing that less than a quarter of the Indiana population over the age of twenty-five has a bachelor's degree or higher.[11] Furthermore, statewide data also revealed that students in the state were struggling with mental health issues, with reports showing that Indiana ranked thirtieth in the nation in the overall well-being of children and youth.[12] Finally, research conducted by the Indiana Chamber of Commerce on behalf of the foundation found that school counseling programs encounter a number of challenges, including high student-to-counselor ratios, countless administrative responsibilities, and inadequate training, among other barriers, that prevent school counselors from effectively serving their students.[13]

The Comprehensive Counseling Initiative, which consists of a $30 million commitment to school counseling, promotes the implementation and development of comprehensive counseling models that address the academic, college, career, and social emotional needs of K–12 students in Indiana.[14] After dedicating $9.4 million to support planning grants for 284 public and charter schools, the foundation has awarded $26.4 million in implementation grants to fifty-two Indiana public schools to enact new school counseling programs and initiatives. The grants, ranging in size from $68,000 to nearly $3 million, are expected to serve 250,000 students in grades K–12.[15]

These funds are being used to increase district capacity and resource alignment to support an effective school counseling program. Some of the strategies these awards are supporting include fostering stronger partnerships and collaboration with mental health providers, business, and university partners; improving the use of digital tools and curricula; and providing professional development to counselors and teachers.

Because the Lilly Endowment fundamentally believes that making sure the conditions are right for school counselors to carry out their work and giving them access to effective tools, resources, partners, and training would better serve students, this initiative is primed to help schools and districts build a system that will work for all students.[16] Accordingly, this initiative is seeking to remove the barriers that counselors face in delivering counseling programs instead of funding a new project that would otherwise provide a temporary solution for the issue. Notably, the foundation identified school leaders' lack of understanding of school counselors' role as one such barrier and, as a result, is allocating a portion of funds to support changes to principal training programs to include more preparation for supporting school counseling.

School districts need to provide vision and support for schools to set up counselors to effectively deliver counseling programs and for school leaders to reinforce this vision at the school level. However, districts need help to create these conditions where they don't already exist. The case of the BPS-AE illustrates this point, as the program's success can be partially attributed to the combination of national and local funding to support infrastructure and capacity building. One year into the grant from EdVestors, Boston Public Schools received a national grant to support this system-level work. The Wallace Foundation, a national funder, was instrumental in supporting the adult development and capacity building that needed to happen at the district level, whereas local funders such as the Barr Foundation and Boston Foundation supported direct arts programming to students. Now, other cities can (and have already started to) visit and learn from BPS-AE so that they can create the changes necessary to grow arts education in their own communities.

Intermediary Organizations

Many successful educational change processes share a common theme: an intermediary organization. The role of EdVestors as an intermediary organization was essential to the district's ability to change its internal structures and processes. The Lilly Endowment enlisted the help of the Indiana Youth Institute to provide technical assistance and coaching during the application process for their Comprehensive Counseling Initiative. Intermediary organizations can play an important mediating role between funders and the recipients of grants. In particular, they are useful in providing fiscal management, offering technical assistance, and creating professional learning communities with shared learning goals. This help is especially useful in the case of foundations that are reluctant to invest directly with school districts due to concerns about the management of funds and limited accountability.

School counselors who are interested in creating system-level change would benefit from investments that bring intermediaries to the table to provide resources and support. As was true in the case of EdVestors, intermediary organizations that have strong relationships with a district are uniquely positioned to successfully push districts to make changes. Because EdVestors had both a track record of helping schools improve and a strong relationship with the Boston Public Schools, the organization took on the role of critical friend. Having both insider and outsider status was instrumental to the systemic change. As an insider, the organization understood the district well and could hold difficult conversations and wield influence. However, an external perspective gave it a unique frame of reference on what was happening in the district. For example, EdVestors was able to collect and share data that compelled the district to act and funders to contribute.

Integrated Funding

One reason the Lilly Endowment sought to improve school counseling in Indiana was the troubling postsecondary metrics (low degree attainment) and social emotional outcomes (overall well-being), both of which fall under counselors' domain. Because of these issues, coupled with research highlighting the impossible conditions in which counselors were attempting to address postsecondary and social emotional outcomes, the foundation elected to see counselors as a lever for change. However, if private philanthropy does not see counselors as instrumental to their existing investments, they are unlikely to invest in the systems that need to be in place for their other investments to work.

One way that foundations can support an academic home framework that enhances student support and development is to include school counselors in preexisting investments. For example, foundations such as the Wallace Foundation and Novo Foundation have heavily invested in social emotional learning. Both of these foundations provide funding to schools and districts to expand opportunities for experiences to promote social emotional learning and skills. Yet, these efforts are generally directed at teachers and, most specifically, elementary school teachers.

While school counselors have yet to be integrated into most recent investments in social emotional learning, they have long been involved in this work. First, school counselors are trained in child and adolescent development and are well suited to deliver social emotional curriculum and support teachers' integration of this content into their curriculum. Second, because social emotional skills are included in the ASCA National Standards, many school counselors are adept at delivering developmental guidance curriculum that cover social emotional content. Private funders who are interested in social emotional development might see counselors in this role and invest in ways to systematically ensure all students benefit from this content. In fact, investing in school counselors at the middle and high school level to carry out this work is especially critical: although most of the social emotional initiatives are focused on elementary ages, research shows these initiatives are just as beneficial for adolescents.

School counselors also have the potential to influence other investments in areas such as mental health, civic education, or even STEM initiatives. For instance, many funders are interested in supporting dropout prevention programs and strategies. Research has pointed to early warning systems, mentoring programs, student engagement activities, career-focused activities, and support for the transition to high school as instrumental to preventing student disengagement from school. School counselors are often centrally involved in carrying out these activities. For instance, middle school counselors spend a lot of time preparing eighth graders for the transition to high school. In fact, middle school counselors have been described as "masters of transition" because of their focus on helping adjust to the demands of high school.[17] Moreover, a lot of their counseling functions are designed to support students' transition from childhood into adolescence. Because of their important role as transition specialists, middle school counselors use a variety of methods to help students develop self-awareness about the many changes going on in schools and their needs. If school counselors are already positioned to influence the things believed to matter to student success, we ought to be investing more in their development and capacity.

POLICY

Similar to the philanthropic changes necessary to support a new vision for school counseling, the ideas in this book also require policy makers to think and act differently. Certainly, state boards or departments of education play a key role in credentialing school counselors and the leaders who support them. However, they also set the stage through other regulatory practices and vision setting for the state. This role includes making changes to state and federal policies such as regulatory requirements, state mandates, and new funding streams.

State Policy

To date, state policies regarding school counseling differ markedly. Some states have passed school counseling mandates requiring counselors in elementary and/or secondary schools, whereas many others have not. Some have passed legislation affecting the funding and the supervision of school counseling, such as mandates about how many observations are needed as part of an evaluation.[18] However, in other states, the school counseling profession is only minimally regulated. This variation creates uneven access to high-quality counseling supports and leaves school and district leaders to make decisions without an understanding of the consequences. Creating a more systematic and effective role for counselors will require this to change.

Because of this research and a growing belief that school counselors play a vital role in supporting the academic, social emotional, and postsecondary development of children, several states are updating policies that influence school counseling programs. Previously, New York mandated neither school counseling for students in grades K–12 nor a specific counseling ratio. However, in response to the New York Department of Education's Every Student Succeeds Act (ESSA) State Plan, which adopts a "Whole School, Whole Community, Whole Child" model to promote positive school climates, the New York Board of Regents recently adopted amendments to the Commissioner's Regulations on school counseling to ensure that all students, especially those in younger grades, have access to a school counselor.[19] These changes will mandate K–12 school counseling programs and require that schools establish a counseling advisory council.

Fortunately, a few states have taken big steps to address gaps in achievement and opportunity through policy changes and grants for school counseling. Colorado is one promising example.

In April 2007, Colorado Governor Bill Ritter created the P-20 Education Coordinating Council, which was tasked with making recommendations for strengthening the state's education system. The council subcommittee on postsecondary preparation was focused on boosting the graduation rate of Colorado high school students as well as the number of students who are prepared for, apply to, and ultimately matriculate at four-year postsecondary institutions.[20] Its members were particularly interested in addressing the state's high student-to-counselor ratio, which at the time exceeded 500:1. Recommendations from this task force led to the creation of the School Counselor Corps Grant Program (SCCGP), a state-funded initiative launched in 2008 that increased the availability of effective school counseling in secondary institutions.[21] The grant provided funding for additional counselors in 126 schools and invested in counselor professional development.

In partnership with the Colorado School Counseling Association, the Colorado Department of Education (CDE) invited proposals from schools, prioritizing those with dropout rates that exceeded the state average or those with a high percentage of students eligible for free or reduced-price lunch.

The schools that were selected are showing impressive gains: after just two years, graduation rates increased by 4.2 percentage points and dropout rates decreased by 3.4 points. Perhaps most notable is the reduced cost to school districts. Assuming that each dropout costs the state $321,450, it is estimated that the SCCGP saved $20 for every

additional $1 invested, equating to a savings so far of $319,842,750.[22]
Based on early assessments, reducing caseloads appears to have been
a worthy investment by the state. Importantly, many attribute the
success of this program to a data-driven model, consistent and mean-
ingful state leadership and support, and attention to accountability.

In addition to ensuring the equitable funding of school counselor positions, state policy can ensure schools provide students an academic home
by mandating that schools have school counseling programs, establishing
maximum student-counselor caseloads, creating infrastructure and leadership, providing training and technical assistance, and including school
counseling in other policy initiatives.

Mandated School Counseling Programs

Not all states mandate school counseling across grade level. For example,
only twenty-seven states plus the District of Columbia have mandated
school counseling for kindergarten through grade eight.[23] A slightly
greater number of states—thirty-two plus the District of Columbia—
have mandated school counseling for grades nine through twelve.[24] Furthermore, *how* these mandates are applied varies by state. For example,
New Jersey, Rhode Island, and Oregon require school counseling programs but do not actually mandate that school counselors be employed,
thereby leaving the door open for other staff to carry out the counseling role. Other states like Virginia have specific guidelines regarding the
number of counselors that must be employed, depending on the size of a
school's student body.[25] Finally, some states like Maine have gone further,
defining what counselors should do and what constitutes a comprehensive guidance program, including the overarching goals of the program
and its implementation timeline.[26] These differences mean that students
in some states are more likely to receive high-quality counseling than students in other states, even when mandates are present.

Along with mandates requiring that counseling programs exist,
schools also can benefit from leadership from the state to provide a clear

vision, rationale, and guidance for how to best implement effective counseling programs. The state of Utah stands out in this regard.

The Utah State Board of Education has a long history of providing leadership to school counseling in the state.[27] The state's first guidance program was implemented in 1986 by Lynn Jensen of the Utah State Office of Education, inspired by the comprehensive school counseling model developed by leading counselor educator Norman Gysbers. Jensen and his colleague, Judy Petersen, drew on implementation science to advance a school counseling agenda in the state that incorporated resources previously allocated to career and technical education. At the time that Jensen and Petersen embarked on what became a long journey, the duo were situated within the state's Career and Technical Education (CTE) department. Because the state had started to look for new ways to improve postsecondary opportunities for students, Jensen and Petersen seized the moment to "take counselors out of their offices and into a new paradigm."

They started by convincing the statewide CTE directors, who represented Utah's forty school districts, to financially support a three-year initiative that would provide intensive training to counselors. By suggesting that districts contribute 8.5 percent of their Perkins funding and that the district CTE director also contribute, they convinced the Utah State Board of Education that they could provide better options for counselors to become brokers of college- and career-readiness information, thereby improving opportunities for postsecondary training and, consequently, strengthening the state economy.[28] Ultimately, the groundswell of interest that followed was the catalyst for what became long-term change.

The first three-year commitment to this initiative included only eleven districts and a yearly summer training that drew counselors, administrators, and district directors. The institute was led by Gysbers, who trained counselors and their role partners in a compre-

hensive counseling model. Ultimately, this institute took place every summer over ten years, funded in its entirety by the state.

Since then, Utah education policy leaders have continually refined the state's school counseling model and hosted a summer statewide training.[29] The latest version of the model, known as the College and Career Readiness School Counseling Program, was designed to expand school counseling beyond secondary school to also recognize the importance of counseling as a form of early intervention in elementary schools.[30]

Today, school counselors in Utah can take a College and Career Readiness course at no cost, thanks to legislative funding. This course, offered as a collaboration between the University of Utah and Utah State University, provides three hours of university credit and, more importantly, gives counselors the knowledge, tools, and skills they need to successfully engage students in planning for life after high school. This, along with the other statewide leadership provided by the Office of Student Success, provides a blueprint for Utah school districts to develop their own vision and support structures for their school counseling programs.

What sets Utah further apart from other states that have not yet taken the steps to mandate the basic expectations for school counseling programs is that the state's mandate is matched by a comprehensive vision and a framework to guide school counseling across the state. In fact, it defines its framework as "student-centered, data-driven, counselor implemented, and systemic in nature."[31] This commitment at the state level sets up counselors as leaders in their state and in their schools and provides resources for counselors to deliver their programming.

Some additional states have begun to take action to include mandates about school counseling in their state regulations, but many have yet to do so. As other states get on board, it will be important that they align new mandates with other policy initiatives while learning from states like

Utah that have built strong infrastructure to help schools and districts meet those mandates.

Mandated Student-Counselor Caseloads

Another way for states to support students' access to school counseling programs and services is through mandated student-counselor caseloads. Mandating maximum caseloads ensures that students have adequate access to a counselor. Implementing an academic home framework where school counselors play a key role in coordination and leadership of a network of people will require that across K–12 caseloads are kept as low as possible to ensure counselors can deliver supports across the three domains.

Mandated caseload policies are driven by research suggesting that lower caseloads are linked to improved outcomes. As noted previously, student-counselor caseloads around the country vary, and in some states, caseloads are very high. Not surprisingly, states with the lowest graduation rates are also those with some of the highest student-to-counselor ratios. As previously mentioned, Arizona has the highest overall student-to-counselor ratio at nearly 903:1 and a graduation rate of only 79.5 percent. Likewise, in the 2015–16 school year, Nevada had a graduation rate of 73.6 percent and a student-to-counselor ratio of 485:1, almost twice the recommended ratio.[32] On the contrary, high-poverty Missouri schools that meet the ASCA-recommended student-to-counselor ratio of 250:1 had significantly higher graduation and attendance rates than similar states with higher ratios.[33] Overall, Missouri has the fifth highest high school graduation rate in the country.[34]

Similar to the mandated counseling program policies, whether and how states regulate caseload size also vary. In total, fourteen states plus the District of Columbia have mandated specific student-to-school counselor ratios, although some mandates are only at the secondary school level; nine states mandate ratios across K–12 while six mandate them for secondary schools (District of Columbia, Louisiana, Mississippi, Nebraska, Oklahoma, and Utah).[35] A number of states have recommended ratios rather than required ratios. For instance, Missouri requires a ratio of 500:1, though it recommends a ratio of 250:1.[36]

A few states with the highest caseloads are beginning to take action to remedy the issue, which is encouraging. For example, the 2009 report *Minnesota's School Counseling Crunch* described how the demands on counselor time have increased at the same time that investments in positions and support have declined. This report, similar to the one that prompted the investment by the Lilly Endowment in Indiana, called on state legislators to reduce the student-to-counselor ratio and to limit counselors' noncounseling and administrative duties. In response, Minnesota Senator Susan Kent coauthored and passed a bill called the Student Support Services Personnel Act that dedicated state funds to hire student support services personnel, including school counselors, psychologists, social workers, nurses, and dependency counselors.[37] This six-year matching grant program required the state to cover half of the cost that districts incur in hiring additional counseling professionals. This cost-sharing model offers a promising way for states to mandate and support caseload maximums.

Research shows that caseloads matter, and we know that schools strapped for time and funding tend to focus on legislative mandates. As mentioned previously, with only fourteen states plus the District of Columbia mandating student-to-school counselor ratios, it is important that other states follow the lead of Minnesota and Missouri to send the message to school districts that keeping caseloads low is critical to student achievement and the long-term health of the state.

Leadership and Infrastructure Support

Mandating school counseling programs and setting caseload maximums are important policies for states to adopt; however, alone, they are not enough. States also need to put leadership in place to create statewide resources, offer technical assistance, and align other statewide policies with a vision for school counseling. Of course, state boards of education are under significant pressure to support numerous mandates with scarce resources, but several states that have made the choice to invest in a school counseling office with dedicated support staff have found that this is money well spent. That is certainly true for the Missouri Department of Elementary and Secondary Education (DESE).

Missouri was one of the first states to systematically recognize and support the work of school counselors. In 1984, the state adopted a comprehensive counseling model.[38] Known today as the Missouri Comprehensive School Counseling Program (MCSCP), the model has four delivery components: school counseling curriculum, responsive services, individual student planning, and system support.[39] At the core of the MCSCP are age-appropriate learning activities that address students' social emotional, academic, and career development.

The state plays an active role in supporting school districts and individual schools with the implementation of the MCSCP. The Missouri Department of Elementary and Secondary Education has a comprehensive website for counselors that includes a school counseling manual, sample lesson plans, resources for conducting program evaluation, and even newsletters with the latest updates from DESE. DESE also supports regional career advisors to work with counselors in developing and implementing individual career and academic plans for students. Finally, DESE invests in the professional development of its counselors, running New Counselor Institutes for novice counselors as well as holding regional trainings and webinars. In partnership with the Missouri School Counselor Association, DESE runs a statewide two-year mentoring program for counselors who are new to the profession. These kinds of investments, combined with state legislation mandating school counseling programs and recommending a ratio of 250:1, provide districts the resources and guidance to ensure students across the state have equal access to an updated school counseling program.

To make mandates effective, state departments need to create structures and employ practices to support districts and schools. Doing so might mean appointing a director or other coordinator of school counseling at the state level. As is the case in Missouri and elsewhere, this professional support could provide leadership for the profession and advocate for policies that are aligned with best practices in the field. For example, statewide school counseling leaders might create resources for counselors to use with their students, such as curriculum for social emotional skills or labor market trends to guide career exploration activities.

State-level leadership can also play a key role in supporting some of the practices called for in this book at the school and district levels. Many states create tools, with input from practicing counselors, for use with students, families, teachers, and even school leaders. For example, previously I described the importance of a principal-counselor agreement for ensuring an aligned relationship and clear expectations. Tennessee is one state in which the statewide school counseling department offers a School Counseling Program Management Agreement. This agreement provides counselors a template to develop and communicate yearly goals and agreed-upon expectations with school leaders. Importantly, when states make these kinds of tools available and collect them, the tools provide states with useful data about what issues counselors are facing and thus what types of additional resources or professional development are needed.

Another strategy that boards of education have employed to make good on legislation is the creation of a statewide school counseling department. The Utah State Board of Higher Education houses a school counseling department that falls under the Student Advocacy Services office and is staffed by three people. The specific department is called School Counseling, Equity and Prevention. In many places, these offices go beyond making resources available to counselors and provide clear direction for how districts should utilize and support counselors. For example, the counseling department also communicates appropriate and inappropriate activities for school counselors, time allocations, and guidance for counselor self-evaluations.

Training and Technical Assistance

State-level leadership and support are especially important to the success of the academic home approach because this high-level perspective ensures that all state policies are designed and implemented with a modern framework for school counselors in mind. Too often, states implement policies that implicate school counselors with little attention to how they will implement them or what additional training is needed. For example, many states have policies that define what constitutes bullying or an unsafe learning environment and outline procedures for reporting bullying. Whereas school counselors may carry out prevention strategies and reporting procedures, these professionals are rarely written into these policies.

The increased use of individualized learning plans (ILPs) offers a good example of why statewide school counseling leadership is instrumental to counselors' practice. Increasingly, states have required middle and/ or high schools to incorporate ILPs into the curriculum.[40] Alternatively known as academic achievement plans, personal learning plans, personal graduation plans, or four-year plans, ILPs are personalized plans for supporting students' achievement as well as college and career readiness.[41] The National Collaborative on Workforce and Disability for Youth suggests that quality ILPs include developing students' self-exploration, career planning and management, and career exploration.[42] Across the country, forty-three states have instituted ILPs; only thirty-three of these states, however, have mandated their implementation.[43] It is important to note that many of the states that mandate ILPs require them only for students in grades nine through twelve, but increasingly states are also implementing them beginning at the eighth-grade level.

ILPs provide both a physically documented plan as well as a process for school counselors and other school professionals to engage with students as they explore their academic, career, and postsecondary options. Given the personalized nature of the ILP, implementing quality ILP programs is time intensive. Many schools have online software that facilitates the implementation of their ILPs, but having counselors meet one on one with students or in small advisory groups regularly throughout the academic year is still a critical facet of this type of program.[44] According to research conducted by the National Association for College Admission Counseling, which surveyed 1,600 school counselors and other school professionals to examine how ILPs function in practice, school counselors were the most likely professionals to be involved in the design, implementation, and evaluation of ILPs.[45] Yet, 44 percent of respondents reported receiving no training prior to implementation. Furthermore, most ILP mandates did not specifically address how states could effectively implement these programs or support the school staff most likely to ensure their effectiveness.

Given the breadth of issues that school counselors are involved in across academic, social emotional, and postsecondary domains, training in various topics is critical to the implementation of various educational policies. This is especially true for those policies for which school counselors act as mediators to their implementation.

The Role of Federal Policy

The federal government also plays a key role in enabling and supporting the implementation of an academic home framework for school counseling in our schools. In fact, as noted previously, federal interest in schools supporting students' career aspirations and plans drove the emergence of the school counseling profession. In recent years, however, the federal government has not invested at the level it once did after the Russian launch of *Sputnik*.

One direct way for the federal government to support the development of an updated vision for school counseling is through grant programs that support counseling programs and professional development. Historically, schools that wished to restructure their current counseling model were able to apply for federal grants that provided essential financial support for new program models through the Elementary and School Counseling Demonstration Program (ESSCP), which was initially introduced through the Elementary School Counseling Demonstration Act of 1995. Through this act, school districts were eligible to receive up to $400,000 per year for a three-year period. These funds could be used for developing or expanding programs that promote students' academic, social emotional, and/or personal growth; providing in-service training for school support staff; hiring additional counselors or school support staff; offering mental health services; and developing links with local social service organizations, higher education institutions, and community organizations to further support students, among other things.[46]

Ultimately, this grant was replaced in the Every Student Succeeds Act (2015) with the Student Support and Academic Enrichment (SSAE) program. SSAE provides funding to local educational agencies to increase student access to a "well-rounded education"; to promote safe, healthy, and drug-free learning environments; and to improve the use of technology to enhance student achievement.[47] School counseling activities that relate to these three areas are authorized to receive funding, though other activities are also eligible for grant support, so districts that want support for the redesign of school counseling programs must compete with other program areas for funding. If states want to support districts, schools, and counselors to enact an academic home framework that can help students meet academic, social emotional, and postsecondary goals, SSAE funds should be focused to support counseling programs specifically.

A different approach by the federal government to support school counseling that does not include providing funds to states or districts is to launch initiatives that encourage and enhance the adoption of aspects of the academic home framework. School districts that create robust data platforms and systems enable school counseling leaders to use that data to inform their programming and how they leverage partners who offer specialized supports. Federal policy and initiatives that focus on making data relevant to school counseling practices accessible and usable are a good example of this. The federal government did just this with the creation of the FAFSA Completion Project.

> In 2010, the US Department of Education launched the Free Application for Federal Student Aid Completion Project to increase the number of high school students who submit the FAFSA. Initially, the program involved only twenty secondary schools and local educational agencies; these schools would submit information about their student body to the US Department of Education's Federal Student Aid (FSA) Office, and in return, the FSA would provide information about whether their students submitted the FAFSA.[48]
>
> In the case of the Albuquerque (New Mexico) School District, one of several districts initially involved in the project, the FSA provided counselors with FAFSA trainings to ensure they had the knowledge and skills needed to support families during the completion initiative.[49] In total, seventy-five high school counselors participated in three-hour trainings. The district also established "trusted centers" in the computer labs of fourteen high schools where students and families could drop in to complete the FAFSA or ask questions. Finally, the school hosted FAFSA completion events. An evaluation of the initiative showed the FAFSA completion rates were ten percentage points higher postintervention.
>
> In March 2012, the project expanded in scope. The Office of Federal Student Aid also released the FAFSA Completion tool that allowed school administrators to access real-time data about FAFSA completions at their institutions.[50] Currently in use today, the tool provides aggregated FAFSA completion data online that is publicly accessible. To receive student-level data, however, high schools and districts must establish an agreement with their state's agency that obtains FAFSA data from the Office of Federal Student Aid.[51] Schools also must have the technical infrastructure to receive, analyze, and store the data.

An important aspect of this initiative is the way this tool has evolved to allow state grant agencies to disclose FAFSA completion information to high schools and other designated entities (e.g., federally funded TRIO or GEAR UP programs) who share an interest in supporting students' postsecondary planning. This data-sharing framework allows schools to safely share data related to FAFSA completion with postsecondary partners who share responsibility for supporting students' completion of this crucial financial application process.

This example of how the federal government can use its influence to create data sources relevant to school counseling practices highlights how changes to the environment in which counseling exists can provide subtle and powerful incentives to encourage data-informed practices. Importantly, in this case, the federal government did not provide direct funding to bolster districts' technical capabilities to take part in the initiative. Although this means that only schools with the technical capacity to send and receive the FAFSA data were eligible to take part in the initiative, it did create an incentive for other school districts to upgrade their data platforms so that they could participate and incorporate this data into their practices. This type of initiative, which facilitates the adoption of key elements of modernized school counseling practices, is another way for the federal government to exert influence on the direction of school counseling programs.

INVESTMENTS IN SCHOOL COUNSELING CHANGE AT SCALE

Changing the system is hard work. In fact, this may be why so many reform efforts focus exclusively on direct services to students. While solely focusing on student-facing practices runs the risk of missing students at critical times, investing in the system can have big pay-offs. According to Marinell Rousmaniere, who led the BPS-AE at EdVestors, one of the most compelling markers for the success of the Boston Public

Schools arts initiative was how a relatively small private investment leveraged significant public investments in arts education. Nine years into their project, the school district had increased its own spending on arts education from $17 million to $26 million annually.[52] As a result, thousands more students have access to sequential arts learning.

Similar to the model of arts education reform utilized by the BPS-AE initiative, school counseling will require philanthropic and public investments to encourage and support the adoption of a new vision. Fortunately, many promising examples of this type of external support for school counseling already underway have addressed capacity building, professional development, and coordination of services. Whether it is in giving seed money to a district to create an action plan or mandating requirements for student-counselor caseloads, these examples highlight the importance of investments that can bring change to scale. Bringing these changes to scale is precisely what is needed to achieve the equity goals that drive our schools, communities, philanthropic partners, and state and federal policy makers.

CONCLUSION

The Case for Equity

Leveraging school counselors to support educational achievement depends on making the crucial work of counselors far more visible. I realized this fact many years ago after I had an experience with a superintendent of a major urban school district. During a keynote address, the superintendent was touting the contributions of a nonprofit organization for its ability to get the district's students into college. The organization was doing such an amazing job, he joked, that it made him wonder if he should cut his counselors and invest the money in the nonprofit.

Surely, this superintendent was being dramatic. However, having heard such sentiments before, I began to imagine what exactly would happen if a district or school lost its counseling positions? Would it, in fact, be better if superintendents reallocated the significant salaries of counselors to support increased nonprofit staffing? Would kids truly be served better?

The superintendent was quick to clarify that, of course, he wouldn't do this because he needed his counselors for "other things." Based on my years working in this field, I knew that this superintendent *did* need his counselors because they were some of the only professionals in his schools focused on academic, social emotional, and postsecondary supports, and chances are, he knew that too. Cutting the counselors would be disastrous, but that fact was not readily apparent to everyone in the audience that day. A deeper understanding of the reality and the promise of the school counseling role is required to realize that while the nonprofit was doing great work in one area, that organization was not creating systemic change. Therefore, removing counselors would illustrate just how many students were not having their needs met by the district's partners alone. The whole conversation ultimately made me wonder: why do districts continue to rely on counselors but fail to empower or support them?

As I have described previously, school counselors can be a valuable resource to tackle education's most pressing issues. Over the past fifty years, schools have been expected to address everything from systemic poverty to concerns about global economic competitiveness. Schools around the country have attempted to keep pace with these expectations through a range of educational reforms, largely focused on instruction, and with the addition of supplemental programs in and out of schools. School counselors have rarely been called on to address these issues. But it doesn't have to be this way.

In this book, I have suggested that educators conceptualize school counseling in a new way. Drawing on the medical home model popularized in health care, I contend that school counselors should be at the center of students' academic, social emotional, and postsecondary development, building on and leveraging other valuable resources inside and outside of schools. The approach of putting counselors in the center to create academic homes builds on work by the American School Counselor Association, Education Trust, National Association for College Admission Counseling, and College Board, which have provided valuable guidance about the day-to-day practices of counselors. Stepping back and putting these pieces into a larger paradigm shift can represent what is possible when we move from seeing counselors as the *problem* to viewing them as part of the *solution*.

AN INVESTMENT IN EQUITY

Choosing to invest time and resources in school counseling is important for all students, but it is especially critical for those who live in and are educated in low-income communities, many of whom are members of racial minority groups. The reality is that the stakes are higher for students who attend under-resourced schools. Many of today's educational reform efforts are aimed at improving instruction with an eye toward increasing the academic performance of students from racial minority groups. Although these reforms have not specifically called for changes in counseling practices, many counselors see this as part of their professional role and are deeply engaged in programming to close this achievement gap. Plenty of research shows that school counselors are especially valuable for first-generation college students' postsecondary planning.[1] However, that is only one small part of a larger issue. In communities where the opioid crisis is hitting hard, where many children are struggling with the conditions related to poverty, or where cases of abuse and neglect are frequent, having access to a counselor is vital to students' success.

Too often, however, these vulnerable students have the least access to high-quality counseling supports. In the United States, 1.6 million students, kindergarten through grade twelve, attend a school with a sworn law enforcement officer but no school counselor, and that is particularly true for students of color. Latino students are 40 percent more likely than white students to attend a school with a sworn law enforcement officer but no school counselor; Asian students are 30 percent more likely; and black students are 20 percent more likely.[2] Ensuring that all students, regardless of race, attend a school with at least one school counselor seems like a low bar and one we need to surpass. Surpassing it means paying attention to inequity in counselor caseloads. It is an outrage that students who attend schools in high poverty neighborhoods and tend to need more support have counselors with, on average, higher caseloads.

Reducing caseloads is only the first step toward equity in counseling, however. The overtaxed and undersupported counselors in high poverty schools also spend less time actually counseling students than those working in high income schools. That point further compromises the already limited access these students have to the supports they need. In a 2012 report published by NACAC, the distribution of time counselors devoted to college counseling differed significantly by high schools' four-year college-going rates. Specifically, counselors from high schools with high college-going rates were more likely to report spending at least 50 percent of their time on college advising tasks.[3] By contrast, nearly three-quarters of counselors from schools with low college-going rates spent less than 20 percent of their time on college counseling. Uneven access to college counseling and advising tilts the playing field in a way that further disadvantages the most vulnerable students. How can we possibly expect low-income and other vulnerable youth to overcome the barriers in their lives and become upwardly mobile when they are moving through inequitable systems of opportunity?

Efforts to close achievement and opportunity gaps need to look closely at the barriers interfering with students' access to counseling. When schools struggle with attendance, for example, they need to see their counselors as critical to the solution—and not just for taking daily attendance and reporting it to the office. In some schools, the solution may mean freeing counselors from administrative or testing responsibilities so that they can conduct home visits, use data to find trends in what groups of students are most absent, or implement classroom lessons that help students see the connection between coming to school and their future. Whatever the approach or specific goal, schools must create the conditions for counselors to address issues of inequality in education.

THE CONDITIONS FOR COUNSELOR SUCCESS

Anyone who has embarked on systemic change knows that everyone in schools needs to play a part for major shifts to take place and for real progress to occur. Counselors are, of course, those most directly affected, but districts, school leaders, and nonprofit partners also play essential roles. Across these diverse roles, the following four principles are essential in guiding school counseling reform:

- Building the counseling community
- Creating a coalition
- Making room for diversity
- Expanding the research base

Building the Counseling Community

At the most fundamental level, we must build the capacity of the professionals doing the work of counseling. Setting the stage for counselors to create strong networks of support and academic homes for students will require us to engage deeply with existing counselors and simultaneously build a pipeline of new counselors.

Prioritizing Professional Training and Support

Bringing the current school counseling workforce into the future vision of the profession will require enhanced professional training and support. Just because counselors want to embrace a new approach does not necessarily mean they have the skills to create and manage networks of support, use data to drive programming, lead teams of people to track student progress, or identify students at risk. Even counselors with training in this area may not be practiced in employing these skills because many schools have not called on them to carry out these tasks. Professional learning organizations might consider offering opportunities that enable counselors to develop the leadership, collaboration, and screening skills that are necessary to operate an academic home. Likewise, counselors would benefit from training and technical assistance that helps them set up the kinds of systems I call for in this book.

Building the community will also require thinking through how we deliver professional development for busy counselors or those who are geographically spread out. In light of the challenges counselors face in accessing professional development due to time and costs, I recommend that professional learning providers experiment with virtual simulations that allow counselors to role play real-world situations as a way to learn

183

new skills. In addition, schools and districts might create online professional learning communities that enable counselors to learn new content in a community of professional peers. Counselors would also benefit from coaches in much the same way that literacy coaches have been used to provide literacy teachers with embedded professional development and support.[4] Coaches could work with teams of counselors, directors of counseling, or individual counselors to bring about the changes or goals needed in specific contexts.

We also need to expand the content of what constitutes professional learning to prepare counselors to lead and manage academic homes with networks of partners. Indeed, when counselors work across multiple domains, as I call for in this book, narrowing the specific scope of content areas that needs to be covered can be difficult. If counselors are simultaneously supporting students who are homeless, contemplating suicide, and experiencing stress at home due to illness, incarceration, or domestic violence, the list of professional development topics is expansive. Instead, professional development should focus on training counselors how to know the signs of emotional or psychological distress and how to connect students to appropriate supports in and out of school. For example, schools have become targets for prevention of and screening for victims of human trafficking. In fact, valuable trainings and resources are available to help schools understand the issue, including what behavioral indicators might signal a student is a victim of sex trafficking.[5] School counselors are among the best suited to receive this training and information to ensure they have a basic understanding of this pervasive issue. However, rather than training counselors in how to support students in these types of situations, the training should focus on screening and how and where to refer potential victims.

Although covering all the topics that intersect in counselors' work is nearly impossible, some topics should be prioritized given the pressing issues in schools and communities today. For example, advocates of career and technical education have argued that school counselors need additional content training in labor market trends and up-and-coming jobs that need to be filled in a twenty-first-century economy. Rarely, if ever, is that content covered in graduate training programs.

One way to bring counselors up to speed on this topic, while also recognizing that local trends differ, is to use "externships." Externships provide valuable exposure to career options and are growing in popularity as a way to expose students (and counselors!) to new career pathways. In response to counselors wishing for training on non-college-going post-secondary options and a growing need in this county for skilled labor, Rouel Belleza, supervisor of student services from Cherokee County School District in Georgia, set up an externship opportunity for his counselors. Over the course of three full days, counselors visited seven work sites across the county. Although each site visit included a glimpse into a different industry, each addressed a coherent set of guiding questions about the transferable skills, internship opportunities for students, and available career pathways at the site and beyond. By visiting each site and, in most cases, engaging in some work onsite, the counselors expanded their knowledge about internships and apprenticeships for students who do not wish to continue formal education beyond high school, a population for which counselors may need assistance. Because he knew that career conversations start early, Belleza intentionally piloted the externship with thirteen counselors spanning elementary, middle, and high schools. Certainly, this is just one example of new topic areas; however, the most important topic areas for professional learning are the ones determined by counselors.

Creating the Pipeline

While strengthening the current counselor workforce is an important step forward, we also need to pay careful attention to recruiting and training a pipeline of new counselors. Currently, the average age of school counselors is 40.5 for female counselors and 43.5 for male counselors.[6] Due to the aging workforce, combined with high burnout rates, the field needs a strong pipeline of highly trained counselors from diverse backgrounds. To date, the field does not mirror student demographics. School counsel-

ing is overwhelmingly dominated by white women, with females repre-
senting 78 percent of the overall school counselor and 77 percent of the
high school counselor populations. Eighty-two percent of counselors at
Title I schools are women. Likewise, 77 percent of counselors identify as
white, 13 percent as Hispanic or Latino, 10 percent as black or African
American, 2 percent as Asian, 1 percent as Native Hawaiian or Pacific
Islander, and 2 percent as American Indian or Alaskan Native. An even
higher percentage of counselors in private schools (83 percent) identify
as white.[7] These statistics, which are not dissimilar from teacher demographics, signal the importance of diversifying the profession. Graduate
schools need to recruit more male counselors and counselors of color.
To do so, counselor education programs might consider partnering with
out-of-school-time and youth development programs to introduce the
possibility of school counseling as a career to these early career professionals. Youth development programs report much more diversity among
racial background and gender and thus may be ideal contexts for recruiting future counselors.

Beyond creating a more diverse cadre of counselors, I recommend
that counselor education programs revisit their curriculum to ensure
that soon-to-be graduates enter the profession ready to advocate for and
work within an academic home approach for counseling. If schools are to
rely on counselors to lead comprehensive support programs for students,
counselor education programs need to align their curriculum to meet the
demands of a renewed role.

With the exception of school counselors working in private schools,
almost 90 percent of school counselors hold a master's degree, largely
in education and counseling.[8] Yet, some educational leaders have questioned the relevance of this training as overemphasizing clinical counseling and underemphasizing educational contexts, college and career
readiness, and leadership. Instead, graduate programs might incorporate coursework on restorative justice practices, using technology in
counseling programs, and personalized learning strategies. In addition,
graduate programs should structure practicum experiences to build the

foundation for counselors' work collaborating with school leaders and colleagues. For example, counselor education programs (which require many hours of field work) might charge preservice counselors with completing counselor-principal agreements or using data-driven school counseling as part of their course assignments.

Building a Coalition

In an academic home approach to counseling, counselors will need to be prepared to meet student and school needs as they evolve, even to address needs we cannot yet anticipate. Accomplishing this will take a commitment from all stakeholders. District and school leaders, teachers, community partners, policy makers, and philanthropists must be ready to keep pace and update expectations, structures, and support. For example, we can make tweaks to improve professional development and develop new curricula, but if school counselors are not on the organizational chart, students will continue to miss out on important supports. However, for the system to change, each constituent needs to do its part.

Training programs for teachers and school leaders can help build a coalition by preparing other preservice educators to support an academic home approach. School leaders, teachers, and other school staff are key partners in an academic home network. Graduate programs must ensure these educators enter the field ready to carry out these roles by incorporating content related to school counseling into their coursework, discussions, and assignments. For educators to work collaboratively in schools, graduate programs should simulate this approach by offering opportunities for them to work alongside one another as part of curricular projects. Given the importance of school leaders to supporting counselors' work, incorporating clear expectations of counselors' role into all preservice training programs is essential. Too often school leaders lack an understanding of school counseling programs and thus struggle in supporting counselors to do their jobs effectively.

At the Harvard Graduate School of Education (HGSE), where I teach, we aim to create shared learning experiences across graduate programs.

A few years ago, my HGSE colleagues and I started hosting a shared learning session for future school leaders and future school counselors aimed at educating each role partner about one another's responsibilities and interests, and to create an opportunity to experience the collaborative relationship we know is essential in the field. Using data from a local district to create a case study about student risk factors, we engaged students in small group collaborative problem solving. We have also created shared learning experiences that bring together future teachers and future counselors to discuss how to best support behavioral challenges in schools. By engaging in a shared learning experience about ways to support students with typical school-based challenges, our preprofessionals discussed how they can work together to support students with behavioral needs.

In the examples of successful school counseling programs in this book, what stands out are schools', districts', and communities' investments in counselors and their work. Counselors need leaders who trust them and hold them to high expectations. This trust allowed Jillian Kelton at TechBoston Academy to develop an intervention team, Toby Marston to develop a new advisory model at Mount Baker High School in Washington, and Nicole Cobb in Nashville to conduct formative evaluations for principals in the Nashville Metro School District. Such trust is built when there are strong relationships between principals and counselors, alignment between counseling programs and schoolwide improvement efforts, and clarity about the kinds of responsibilities that leaders should (and should not) expect counselors to assume.

Trust is also essential to support working relationships between school counselors and their community-based program partners. One way to achieve this trust is to offer shared professional learning. To date, school counselors and their colleagues attend professional development separately. Often nonprofit organizations host professional learning events that could be opened up to school counselors. Likewise, districts might consider inviting community-based partners to district-sponsored professional trainings.

Another way to promote collaborative, trusting relationships between counselors and their community partners is for community organizations to carefully plan their entry into school partnerships. For example, when nonprofit programs train staff to work in schools, managers should be clear about how their role is different from school counselors and how they can work in partnership with school-based support staff. I know some community organizations that bring school counselors into their yearly training programs to introduce staff to the role of counselors and what makes for a successful partnership. This type of introduction is especially important in programs that originated as a way to compensate for weak school-based counseling supports and, as a result, might unintentionally perpetuate a negative, single story of school counselors that could shape the stereotypes of counselors that staff hold.

As educational leaders change the way they think about and support school counseling, counselors also need to be ready to play an active role in bringing about change and bringing others on board. This means counselors need to be open to trying new ways of working, temporarily giving up time with students to create systems, and trusting others in their network. They also need to communicate and advocate for their new roles. Indeed, within the school counseling profession, communication is as important as relationships. According to researchers Aviva Shimoni and Lori Greenberger, when school counselors communicate their professional role to various stakeholders outside the profession, they are more effective in their work.[9] These researchers contend that school counselors are better positioned to advocate for students or groups of students, for specific programming, or even for policy change when key stakeholders understand the function of the profession.[10]

Whether it is with school leaders, families, or the general public, school counselors should experiment with new forms of communicating their role. To capitalize on others' willingness to invest in counseling, school counselors need to present themselves as highly capable and instrumental to schoolwide goals and student success. Shimoni and Greenberger suggest that school counselors need to give up their "professional modesty" and communicate "who they are, what they do, and their professional identity."[11] When everyone in a student's ecology communicates clearly about appropriate role expectations, there is more trust and effective collaboration. Importantly, the more people in a student's ecology who understand counselors' role, the more that message will be delivered to students. Although some educators may feel that communicating their work will be perceived as boastful or a waste of time, this could not be further from the truth. The fact remains that school counselors' unique function has continued to be a mystery to most educators. Communication and clarity of role is an essential step in building the kinds of relationships that support an academic home.

Making Room for Diversity

One of the benefits of proposing a new approach, rather than a prescribed model, is that it allows for plenty of differentiation depending on context. Generally speaking, the scope of counseling (academic, social emotional, and college and career supports) is consistent across the profession. However, how counselors work in each of these domains is different by grade level, geographic location, and student populations. Differences also emerge in relation to other contextual variables, such as the availability of community partners and school resources. These differences are important to keep in the front of our minds when considering how to put counselors in the center of student support programming. Just like teachers differentiate their instruction, counselors need to differentiate their services and interventions based on student and community needs.

For example, school counselors in elementary and middle schools engage in a lot of consultation and coordination. In addition to partnering with teachers, elementary school counselors can also be found conducting small group or individual counseling and leading classroom lessons. These counselors often use classroom settings to teach children about age-appropriate issues such as fairness, tattling, and bullying, and deliver lessons to promote social emotional skills such as expressing their feelings. Likewise, middle school counselors spend much of their time running group counseling sessions for children with common needs, such as those grappling with divorce or living with a family member who is ill. However, high school counselors may not spend as much time in groups and instead spend more time individually with students on similar types of issues. Instead of group sessions on elementary issues, the work of secondary counselors may be more focused on topics such as racial identity development or perceptions of school belonging.

Supporting the differentiated application of the ideas in this book is especially important for counselors working in different geographic settings. Specific counselor practices are guided by unique student needs, availability of resources, parenting styles and expectations, and community norms, all of which vary by community context. School counselors in rural communities, for example, are likely supporting some students who experience both the psychological and interpersonal stressors that are unique to living in a rural community (e.g., low employment, limited resources) and benefitting from the assets of living in such a community (e.g., strong community relationships, tight culture, strong connection between school and community). Additionally, some rural school counselors work across K–12, which means their efforts must take into account multiple developmental levels and, sometimes, working in multiple buildings.

Expanding the Research Base

While existing school counseling research makes a strong case for investing in a change process, school counselors and their partners will require more evidence of the innovative practices highlighted in this book and beyond. By now, you are likely convinced that school counselors have an impact on students' lives. But *why* and *how* are harder questions to answer. In part, articulating succinctly why counselors matter to students is challenging because their influence spans the academic, social emotional, and postsecondary domains described already. Unfortunately, current scholarship is this field is limited. Though many outside the field of counseling investigate issues germane to school counseling (i.e., higher education researchers, economists, psychologists), their lack of perspective on the profession limits the relevance and applicability of their findings to counseling practice. Of course, most school counselors are too busy doing the work to conduct research or document and disseminate their innovative practices.

Counselor educators at the University of Massachusetts at Amherst are actively trying to close the gap between school counseling research and action. Through the Ronald H. Fredrickson Center for School Counseling Outcome Research and Evaluation (CSCORE), researchers are committed to ensuring that the benefits of effective counseling are clear. Carey Dimmitt, John Carey, and their colleagues have partnered with several state departments to measure and evaluate school counselor effectiveness and advance school counseling research. Research from this center, and that by other school counseling scholars, can play a pivotal role in documenting how collaborative approaches lead to improved outcomes. As the research base on school counseling expands, scholars should explore what models work and under what conditions so that they can be easily replicated.

Still, counseling educators contend that the scarcity of literature on counselor impact is exacerbated by the fact that such research is expensive and philanthropy and federal agencies have not funded many studies about school counseling. As districts and schools experiment with new models, these efforts should be documented, evaluated, and communicated to broad audiences. Often, funders preference innovative practices that have been evaluated and communicated through publications. This point was recently driven home to me in a conversation with a national funder who was looking for promising evidence-based practices related to college readiness. As part of my research for this book, I knew that promising examples of school counseling initiatives could be effectively scaled. Unfortunately, these bright spots are rarely documented in a way that elicits philanthropic interest. Together, counselor educators, educational researchers, and private funders can correct this trend so the good work that is happening can reach more schools and ultimately benefit more students.

READY FOR CHANGE

As schools stretch to address calls for increasing academic standards and achievement, attending to students' social emotional needs, and preparing students for career and college success, school counselors are ready and willing to be part of the solution. As this book shows, counselors are valuable assets to school and district leaders who are committed to advancing students' success across academic, social emotional, and postsecondary domains. However, leveraging all they have to offer will take making change to our current approach to school counseling. With the preceding principles in mind, now is the right moment to create systemic change, and I believe counselors, school leaders, and their educational partners are ready for that change. Too often, I have found myself speaking with school and district leaders, policy makers, and others outside the school counseling profession who simply can't understand why things aren't working better than they are. They know we need to make change but are not sure where to start. As a school counselor at heart, I wrote this book to help educational constituents see what I see—that there is so much possibility. I wanted to highlight the bright spots and encourage others to learn from them. I also wanted to show that improving school counseling is a shared responsibility that goes well beyond the school counseling community.

Fostering an academic home that draws on the unique contributions of many partners depends on a strong collaborative system, and that system starts with school and district leaders and depends on support from policy makers and philanthropists. The examples I have highlighted illustrate what is possible when school districts place counselors in leadership roles; hold them to high expectations; and enable them to organize, manage, and deliver counseling programs with the help of their partners, data systems, and strong professional development programs. For some educators, applying the concepts of an academic home will mean making changes to how a counseling department is structured or hiring an additional counselor, whereas for others, it might mean a major overhaul to how a district operates. We can all draw from these examples to create scalable changes. Beyond a single school example or single story, we can all be inspired to think differently.

Recently, important seeds have been planted for reimagining the profession, and school counselors are ready to seize a twenty-first-century *Sputnik*-like moment. In 2014, First Lady Michelle Obama launched her Reach Higher initiative aimed at inspiring more Americans to continue their education beyond high school. Among Reach Higher's four primary components, the initiative stressed the importance of school counselors as instrumental in providing postsecondary supports, especially for those who are first in their families to attend college. This was the first time in over fifty years that counselors were called on to be part of a national change initiative. The groundswell of interest that followed demonstrated just how ready counselors are for change.

Because of her personal experience as a first-generation college graduate and her steadfast belief in the power of education, Mrs. Obama launched the Reach Higher initiative to support President Obama's goal of more Americans attaining a post-high school credential. Reach Higher was not the only initiative supporting this goal, but what stands out about it is the former First Lady's decision to use school counseling as a lever to achieve this goal. When she learned that in some states school counselors were responsible for over eight hundred students and that in some schools counselors were assigned so many noncounseling duties that they had little time to spend with students, she saw the weakness in our current system and chose to tackle that issue. Choosing to focus on a problem in our current model illustrated the former First Lady's commitment to all children.

Reach Higher was not the first time Michelle Obama took on an intractable systems issue. As part of her signature public health campaign to reduce childhood obesity, Let's Move, the former First Lady spearheaded initiatives to create school lunch standards and to add sixty minutes of physical exercise into the school day. She knew that unless we changed the system we already have in place, equalizing opportunity would be well beyond her reach. Ultimately, she challenged the system to do better. In many ways, the Reach Higher focus on school counseling brought forth a similar challenge.

In interviews with and articles written by Mrs. Obama, one learns that her personal story drives her as much as her interest in national degree attainment. As a young woman from the south side of Chicago, she knows firsthand about disproportionate opportunities. And, because she wants all young people in the nation to have access to the kinds of educational opportunities she had, she believes that students should not have to compete with eight hundred peers or administrative duties for time with a counselor. The former First Lady saw school counseling as a powerful lever for increasing the number of Americans with postsecondary credentials. By putting a spotlight on school counseling; honoring the School Counselor of the Year similar to how the White House has honored the Teacher of the Year; and using her bully pulpit to compel schools, universities, and nonprofit organizations to do more and behave differently, she changed the conversation on college going in America. Importantly, she added school counselors to that conversation. She made sure everyone understood that high caseloads, poor training, and misuse of counselors could not remain.

In small but important ways, Reach Higher has started to have an impact on system-level change in school counseling. From social media to star-studded School Counselor of the Year awards, more attention than ever is focused on school counseling. At a Harvard Graduate School of Education convening in 2014 to support the then First Lady's initiative, school counselors, counselor educators, district leaders, nonprofit leaders, policy makers, and other influential stakeholders gathered to share best practices and make specific, actionable commitments for supporting counselors. The convening was followed by many more national, regional, and state-level convenings—across the span of only three and a half years. Together, these convenings galvanized counselors and their partners who are ready to make changes to school counseling and college counseling around the country. Now, it is time we get the rest of educational system on board.

However, seizing this call to action and realizing change depends on others joining in the coalition. It depends on all of us who work in and around counseling to see the possibilities and make them realities. If we truly want schools to be places where children and youth can reach their fullest potential as students, learners, citizens, and humans, we need to recommit to the vital school-based supports that are needed in today's world. We need to avoid the temptation to see a system broken beyond repair and instead reimagine the possibilities of a strong school counseling program. We need to raise our expectations of school counselors and their value to our school communities and students. This reconceptualization places responsibility on all educators to create the conditions for counselors to provide the support our students need and woefully deserve. When we accept responsibility for these changes, we will take an important leap forward in fulfilling the promise of educational opportunity that we make to our students every day.

NOTES

Introduction

1. Susan Williams White and F. Donald Kelly, "The School Counselor's Role in School Dropout Prevention," *Journal of Counseling & Development* 88, no. 2 (2010): 227–28; Jonathan Ohrt, Lindsay Webster, and Mario De La Garza, "The Effects of a Success Skills Group on Adolescents' Self-Regulation, Self-Esteem, and Perceived Learning Competence," *Professional School Counseling* 18, no. 1 (2015): 174–75; Greg Brigman and Chari Campbell, "Helping Students Improve Academic Achievement and School Success Behavior," *Professional School Counseling* 7, no. 2 (2003): 96–97.

2. Carey Dimmit and Belinda Wilkerson, "Comprehensive School Counseling in Rhode Island: Access to Services and Student Outcomes," *Professional School Counseling* 16, no. 2 (2012): 129–32; Sharon M. Schlossberg, John D. Morris, and Mary G. Lieberman, "The Effects of a Counselor-Led Guidance Intervention on Students' Behaviors and Attitudes," *Professional School Counseling* 4, no. 3 (2001): 161–62.

3. Michael Hurwitz and Jessica Howell, "Estimating Causal Impacts of School Counselors with Regression Discontinuity Designs," *Journal of Counseling & Development* 92, no. 3 (2014): 322; Erin Dunlop Velez, *How Can High School Counseling Shape Students' Postsecondary Attendance? Exploring the Relationship Between the High School Counseling Context and Students' Subsequent Postsecondary Enrollment* (Arlington, VA: National Association for College Admission Counseling, 2016), 2.

4. Andrew Ujifusa, "How Do Districts Plan to Use Their ESSA Block Grant Money?" *Education Week,* June 17, 2018, http://blogs.edweek.org/edweek/campaign-k-12/2018/06/essa_title_iv_block_grant_stem_school_safety_technology.html?cmp=soc-twitter-shr.

5. Bureau of Labor Statistics, "Occupational Employment and Wages, May 2017: 21-1012 Educational, Guidance, School, and Vocational Counselors," https://www.bls.gov/oes/current/oes211012.htm#nat.

6. US Department of Education, National Center for Education Statistics, Common Core of Data, "State Nonfiscal Public Elementary/Secondary Education Survey Directory Data," 2015-16 V.1a.

7. American School Counselor Association, *Student-to-School Counselor Ratio 2015–2016* (Alexandria, VA: ASCA, 2018), 1.

8. Richard T. Lapan et al., "Missouri Professional School Counselors: Ratios Matter, Especially in High-Poverty Schools," *Professional School Counseling* 16, no. 2 (2012): 111–13.

9. The College Board National Office for School and Counselor Advocacy, *The College Board 2012 National Survey of School Counselors and Administrators: Report on Survey Findings:*

Barriers and Supports to School Counselor Success (Washington, DC: NOSCA, 2012), 29.

10. The term *noncognitive* describes the range of behaviors, mindsets, and developmental skills that are conducive to college and career success. Despite criticisms that the term is misleading, I use it here because of its popularity and wide relevance in education.

11. PBIS, or Positive Behavioral Intervention and Supports, is a strengths-based, proactive approach to implementing behavioral supports for students using evidence-based practices.

12. Emily Goodman-Scott, "Maximizing School Counselors' Efforts by Implementing Schoolwide Positive Behavioral Interventions and Supports: A Case Study from the Field," *Professional School Counseling* 17, no. 1 (2013): 111–12.

13. Patricia Van Velsor, "School Counselors as Social-Emotional Learning Consultants: Where Do We Begin?" *Professional School Counseling* 13, no. 1 (2009): 53–54.

14. Maurice J. Elias, "In Defense of School Counseling," *Edutopia*, May 13, 2010, https://www.edutopia.org/school-counseling-importance-of-elias.

15. Lorraine Dekruyf, Richard W. Auger, and Shannon Trice-Black, "The Role of School Counselors in Meeting Students' Mental Health Needs: Examining Issues of Professional Identity," *Professional School Counseling* 16, no. 5 (2013): 272.

16. National Assessment of Educational Progress, "2015: Mathematics & Reading at Grade 12," https://www.nationsreportcard.gov/reading_math_g12_2015/#/.

17. Greg A. Brigman, Linda D. Webb, and Chari Campbell, "Building Skills for School Success: Improving the Academic and Social Competence of Students," *Professional School Counseling* 10, no. 3 (2007): 283–85.

18. These are just four examples of recent trends in education that profile the key role of school counselors; however, school counselors' work is nested in schools in a way that positions them to address an even wider range of issues, from prevention and programming to crisis response.

19. Jean Johnson et al., *Can I Get a Little Advice Here* (Brooklyn, NY: Public Agenda, 2010), 10.

20. US Department of Education, Office for Civil Rights, *A First Look: Key Data Highlights on Equity and Opportunity Gaps in Our Nation's Public Schools* (Washington, DC: US Department of Education, 2016), 1.

21. Douglas J. Gagnon and Marybeth J. Mattingly, *Most U.S. Districts Have Low Access to School Counselors,* National Issue Brief #108 (Durham, NH: University of New Hampshire, Carsey School of Public Policy, 2016), 2.

22. Alexandria Walton Radford and Nicole Ilfill, *Preparing Students for College: What High Schools Are Doing and How Their Actions Influence Ninth Graders' College Attitudes, Aspirations and Plans* (Arlington, VA: National Association for College Admission Counseling, 2012), 8.

23. Phi Delta Kappan, *The 49th Annual PDK Poll of the Public's Attitudes Toward the Public Schools* (Arlington, VA: Phi Delta Kappan, 2017), K10.

Chapter 1

1. George E. Myers, "A Critical Review of Present Developments in Vocational Guidance with Special Reference to Future Prospects," *The Vocational Guidance Magazine,* 2 (1923): 140.

2. For a more detailed discussion of the history of the school counseling profession, several resources are available, including Sejal Parikh Foxx, Stanley B. Baker, and Edwin R. Gerler, Jr., *School Counseling in the 21st Century* (New York: Routledge, 2017); John J. Schmidt, "History of School Counseling," in *Handbook of School Counseling,* eds. Hardin L. K. Coleman and Christine Yeh (Abingdon, UK: Routledge, 2008), 3–13.

3. Melissa Clinedinst and Anna-Maria Koranteng, *2017 State of College Admission* (Arlington, VA: National Association for College Admission Counseling, 2017), 24.

4. Frank Parsons, *Choosing a Vocation* (Boston: Houghton Mifflin, 1909), 4.

5. National Vocation Act, Pub. L. No. 64-367, 39 Stat. 929 (1917).

6. Vocational Act of 1946, 20 U.S.C. § 11 (1969).

7. Nancy Conneely et al., "School Counselors as CTE Stakeholders," June 2009, https://cte.careertech.org/sites/default/files/CounselorsasCTEStakeholders-June2009.pdf.

8. Carey Dimmit and Belinda Wilkerson, "Comprehensive School Counseling in Rhode Island: Access to Services and Student Outcomes," *Professional School Counseling* 16, no. 2 (2012): 129–32.

9. Centers for Disease Control and Prevention, "Mental Health Surveillance Among Children—United States, 2005–2011," *Morbidity and Mortality Weekly Report* 62, no. 2 (2012): 1–37; Howard S. Adelman and Linda Taylor, "Mental Health in Schools: Moving in New Directions," *Contemporary School Psychology,* 16 (2012): 9.

10. Kathleen R. Merikangas et al., "Lifetime Prevalence of Mental Disorders in U.S. Adolescents: Results from the National Comorbidity Survey Republication-Adolescent Supplement (NCS-A)," *Journal of the American Academy of Child and Adolescent Psychiatry* 49, no. 10 (2010): 985.

11. Terese J. Lund and Eric Dearing, "Growing Up Affluent Risky for Adolescents or Is the Problem Growing Up in an Affluent Neighborhood?" *Journal of Research on Adolescence* 23, no. 2 (2012): 279–80.

12. American School Counselor Association, *The School Counselor and Student Mental Health* (Alexandria, VA: ASCA, 2015), 57–59.

13. Anne Erickson and Nicholas R. Abel, "A High School Counselor's Leadership in Providing School-wide Screenings for Depression and Enhancing Suicide Awareness," *Professional School Counseling* 16, no. 5 (2013): 284.

14. Phyllis J. Hart and Maryann Jacobi, *From Gatekeeper to Advocate: Transforming the Role of the School Counselor* (New York: College Entrance Examination Board, 1992), 7.

15. Commission on Precollege Guidance and Counseling, *Keeping the Options Open: Recommendations. Final Report of the Commission on Precollege Guidance and Counseling* (New York: College Board, 1987), 16–18.

16. President Barack Obama, "Remarks of President Barack Obama—Address to Joint Session of Congress" (Speech, Washington, DC, February 24, 2009), The White House,https://obamawhitehouse.archives.gov/the-press-office/remarks-president-barack-obama-address-joint-session-congress.

17. American School Counseling Association, "ASCA and Reach Higher," https://www.schoolcounselor.org/school-counselors-members/legislative-affairs/asca-and-reach-higher.

18. Reach Higher, *Reach Higher Progress Report* (Washington, DC: Reach Higher, 2017), 4.

19. Andrew S. Belasco, "Creating College Opportunity: School Counselors and Their Influence on Postsecondary Enrollment," *Research in Higher Education* 54, no. 7 (2013): 781–804.

20. Margaret Cahalan and David Goodwin, *Setting the Record Straight: Strong Positive Impact Found from the National Evaluation of Upward Bound* (Washington, DC: The Pell Institute, 2014), 14–21.

21. US Department of Education, *50th Anniversary Federal TRIO Programs Fact Sheet* (Washington, DC: US Department of Education, 2016), 11.

22. Matthew M. Chingos, "No More Free Lunch for Education Policymakers and Researchers," *Evidence Speaks Reports* 1, no. 20 (2016): 2.

23. Patricia M. McDonough, *Choosing Colleges: How Social Class and Schools Structure Opportunity* (Albany: State University of New York Press, 1997), 151.

24. American School Counselor Association, *The School Counselor's Role in Educational Reform* (Alexandria, VA: ASCA, 1994).

25. The National Center for Transforming School Counseling, "The New Vision for School Counselors: Scope of the Work," http://edtrust.org/wp-content/uploads/2014/09/TSC-New-Vision-for-School-Counselors.pdf.

26. Many counselor education programs today train school counselors with this curricular focus.

27. No Child Left Behind Act, 20 U.S.C. §6301 (2001).

28. Tina R. Paone and William J. Lepkowski, "No Childhood Left Behind: Advocating for the Personal and Social Development of Children," *Journal of School Counseling* 5, no. 25 (2007): 3.

29. Catherine L. Dimmitt, John C. Carey, and Patricia A. Hatch, *Evidence-Based School Counseling: Making a Difference with Data-Driven Practices* (Thousand Oaks, CA: Corwin Press, 2007), 3.

30. Thomas L. Sexton, "Evidence-Based Counseling: Implications for Counseling Practice, Preparation, and Professionalism," *ERIC Digest* EDO-CG-99-9 (1999): 1.

31. John C. Carey et al., "Report of the National Panel for Evidence-Based School Counseling: Outcome Research Coding Protocol and Evaluation of Student Success Skills and Second Step," *Professional School Counseling* 11, no. 3 (2008): 197.

32. Dimmitt, Carey, and Hatch, *Evidence-Based School Counseling*, 4.

33. John Carey, Karen Harrington, Ian Martin, and Dawn Stevenson, "A Statewide Evaluation of the Outcomes of the Implementation of ASCA National Model School Counseling Programs in Utah High School," *Professional School Counseling* 16, no. 2 (2012): 95; Holly Kayler and Jamie Sherman, "At-Risk Ninth-Grade Students: A Psychoeducational Group Approach to Increase Study Skills and Grade Point Averages," *Professional School Counseling* 12, no. 6 (2009): 436–37; Jonathan Ohrt, Lindsay Webster, and Mario De La Garza, "The Effects of a Success Skills Group on Adolescents' Self-Regulation, Self-Esteem, and Perceived Learning Competence," *Professional School Counseling* 18, no. 1 (2015): 174–75.

34. Norman C. Gysbers, *Comprehensive Guidance Programs That Work* (Washington, DC: ERIC Counseling and Personnel Services Clearinghouse, 1990), 17.

35. For a detailed summary of the ASCA model, see American School Counselor Association, *ASCA National Model: A Framework for School Counseling Programs Executive Summary*, 3rd ed. (Alexandria, VA: ASCA, 2012); Carol A. Dahir, "School Counseling: Moving Toward Standards and Models," in *Handbook of School Counseling*, eds. Hardin L. K. Coleman and Christine Yeh (Abingdon, UK: Routledge, 2008), 34–37.

36. American School Counselor Association, "State School Counseling Programs & Web Sites," https://www.schoolcounselor.org/school-counselors-members/careers-roles/state-school-counseling-programs-web-sites; American School Counselor Association, *The School Counselor and Comprehensive School Counseling Programs* (Alexandria, VA: ASCA, 2012), 11.

37. Leona E. Tyler, *The National Defense Counseling and Guidance Training Institutes Program: A Report of the First 50 Institutes*, Bulletin No. 31, OE-25011 (Washington, DC: US Department of Health, Education, and Welfare, Office of Education, 1960), 12.

38. John J. Schmidt, "History of School Counseling," in *Handbook of School Counseling*, eds. Hardin L. K. Coleman and Christine Yeh (Abingdon, UK: Routledge, 2008), 8.

39. Patricia J. Martin, "Transforming School Counseling: A National Perspective," *Theory Into Practice* 51, no. 3 (2002): 148; Reese M. House and Susan Jones Sears, "Preparing School Counselors to Be Leaders and Advocates: A Critical Need in the New Millennium," *Theory Into Practice*, 41, no. 3 (2002): 158–61.

40. The DeWitt Wallace-Reader's Digest Fund, known today as the Wallace Foundation, is a philanthropy established by the original founders of The Readers Digest Association, DeWitt and Lila Acheson Wallace. The Wallace Foundation supports programs for disadvantaged youth as well as various cultural and artistic causes; Martin, "Transforming School Counseling," 148.

41. John Bridgeland and Mary Bruce, *2011 National Survey of School Counselors: Counseling at a Crossroads* (Washington, DC: The College Board National Office for School Counselor Advocacy, 2011), 28.

42. Abby Miller, Ashley Ison, Thad Bowman, and Samantha Richardson, *Building College Access/Admission Counseling Competencies: Review of the Coursework* (Arlington, VA:

The Council of National School Counseling & College Access Organizations, 2016), 15.

43. Sejal Parikh Foxx, Stanley B. Baker, and Edwin R. Gerler, Jr., *School Counseling in the 21st Century* (New York: Routledge, 2017), 24.

44. Foxx, Baker, and Gerler, *School Counseling*, 24.

45. Dahir, "School Counseling," 37.

46. Michelle Obama, "Remarks by the First Lady at the School Counselor of the Year" (Speech, Washington, DC, January 28, 2016), The White House, https://obamawhitehouse.archives.gov/the-press-office/2016/01/28/remarks-first-lady-school-counselor-year.

Chapter 2

1. Unlike similar-styled vignettes in this book, this case example is based on a real student. However, I have used a pseudonym to protect her identity.

2. Although this particular student's experience in foster care was not ideal, I worked with many students who found loving homes in foster care and with foster families. Thus, I want to be cautious about conveying a single idea about foster care experiences in sharing this story.

3. Barbara Starfield and Thomas Oliver, "Primary Care in the United States and Its Precarious Future," *Health and Social Care in the Community* 7, no. 5 (1999): 315.

4. American Academy of Family Physicians, *Primary Care for the 21st Century: Ensuring a Quality, Physician-Led Team for Every Patient* (Leawood, KS: AAFP, 2012), 4.

5. Patient-Centered Primary Care Collaborative, *The Impact of Primary Care Practice Transformation on Cost, Quality, and Utilization* (Washington, DC: PCPCC, 2017), 4–5.

6. American Academy of Family Physicians, *Primary Care for the 21st Century*, 4.

7. Health Innovation Network, *What Is Person-Centered Care and Why Is It Important?* (London, United Kingdom: Health Innovation Network, 2016), 2.

8. Patricia M. McDonough, *Choosing Colleges: How Social Class and Schools Structure Opportunity* (Albany: State University of New York Press, 1997), 151.

9. Mary Walsh and Joan Wasser Gish, "Improving Student Achievement by Meeting Children's Comprehensive Needs," in *Memos to the President on the Future of U.S. Education Policy*, ed. Michael Hansen and Jon Valant (Washington, DC: Brookings Institution, 2016), 1; Coalition for Community Schools, *What Is a Community School?* (Washington, DC: Coalition for Community Schools, Institute for Educational Leadership, 2014), 1.

10. Agency for Healthcare Research and Quality, "Defining the PCMH," https://pcmh.ahrq.gov/page/defining-pcmh.

11. Franciene S. Sabens and Brett Zyromski, "Aligning School Counselors, Comprehensive School Counseling Programs, and the No Child Left Behind Act of 2001," *Journal of School Counseling* 7, no. 31 (2009): 24.

12. American School Counselor Association, *ASCA National Model: A Framework for School Counseling Programs*, 3rd ed. (Alexandria, VA: ASCA, 2012), 1.

13. Randall L. Astramovich, "Program Evaluation Interest and Skills of School Counselors," *Professional School Counseling* 20, no. 1 (2016): 61.

14. Dee Hann-Morrison, "The Varied Roles of School Counselors in Rural Settings," *Georgia School Counselors Association* 18, no. 1 (2011): 26.

15. US Department of Education, National Center for Education Statistics, Common Core of Data, "State Nonfiscal Public Elementary/Secondary Education Survey Directory Data," 2015-16 V.1a.

16. US Department of Education, "Education Survey Directory Data."

17. World Health Organization, *The World Health Report 2008: Primary Health Care Now More Than Ever Before* (Geneva, Switzerland: WHO, 2008), 48.

Chapter 3

1. For a detailed description of Mount Baker High School's transformation process, read Diana H. Gruman, Toby Marston, and Holly Koon, "Bringing Mental Health Needs into Focus Through School Counseling Program Transformation," *Professional School Counseling* 16, no. 5 (2013): 338–39.

2. Jason E. Harlacher, Tami L. Sakelaris, and Nicole M. Kattelman, *Practitioner's Guide to Curriculum-Based Evaluation in Reading* (New York: Springer, 2014), 23.

3. Harlacher, Sakelaris, and Kattelman, *Practitioner's Guide*, 30.

4. Katie Martens and Kelsey Andreen, "School Counselors' Involvement with a School-wide Positive Behavior Support System: Addressing Student Behavior Issues in a Proactive and Positive Manner," *Professional School Counseling* 16, no. 5 (2013): 314.

5. Harlacher, Sakelaris, and Kattelman, *Practitioner's Guide*, 30.

6. Trish Hatch, "Multi-Tiered, Multi-Domain System of Supports," *Hatching Results,* March 8, 2017, https://www.hatchingresults.com/blog/2017/3/multi-tiered-multi-domain-system-of-supports-by-trish-hatch-phd.

7. David Allen et al., *Supporting Students' Success Through Distributed Counseling: A Core Principle for Small Schools* (Princeton, NJ: Institute for Student Achievement, 2006), 2.

8. National Middle School Association, NMSA Research Summary # 9: Advisory Programs, http://www.ncmle.org/research%20summaries/ressum9.html.

9. Vincent A. Anfara, Jr., *Research Summary: Advisory Programs* (Westerville, OH: NMSA, 1999), 1.

10. Carnegie Council on Adolescent Development, *Turning Points: Preparing American Youth for the 21st Century. The Report of the Task Force on Education of Young Adolescents* (New York: Carnegie Corporation, 1989), 40.

11. Charles Tocci and David Allen, *Practice Brief #2: Key Dimensions in Advisory Programs* (New York: NCREST, 2008), 1; Sally N. Clark and Donald C. Clark, *Restructuring the Middle Level School: Implications for School Leaders* (Albany, NY: State University of New York, 1994), 134–35.

12. Rachel A. Poliner and Carol Miller Lieber, *The Advisory Guide: Designing and Implementing Effective Advisory Programs in Secondary Schools* (Cambridge, MA: Educators for Social Responsibility, 2004), 56–57.
13. Josephine Imbimbo, Samuel Morgan, and Eileen Plaza, *Center for School Success Promising Practices Series: Student Advisory* (New York: New Visions for Public Schools, 2009), 2.
14. Imbimbo, Morgan, and Plaza, *Center for School Success*, 3.
15. Poliner and Miller Lieber, *The Advisory Guide*, 46.
16. John P. Galassi, Suzanne A. Gulledge, and Nancy D. Cox, *Advisory: Definitions, Descriptions, Decisions, Directions* (Westerville, OH: National Middle School Association, 1998), 46.
17. Watson Scott Swail, "Preparing America's Disadvantaged for College: Programs That Increase College Opportunity," *New Directions for Institutional Research* 27, no. 3 (2000): 91–92.
18. Centers for Disease Control and Prevention, *Results from the School Health Policies and Practices Study 2016* (Washington, DC: National Center for HIV/AIDS, Viral Hepatitis, STD, and TB Prevention, Division of Adolescent and School Health, 2013), 36.
19. Centers for Disease Control and Prevention, *Results from the School Health Policies*, 49.
20. Centers for Disease Control and Prevention, 50.
21. Boston Children's Hospital Neighborhood Partnerships Program, "Training and Access Project," http://www.childrenshospital.org/centers-and-services/programs/a-_-e/boston-childrens-hospital-neighborhood-partnerships-program/training-and-access-project.
22. Personal interview with Janice Bloom, June 8, 2018.
23. College Access: Research & Action, "Right to College," https://caranyc.org/right-to-college/.
24. Lori Chajet and Lisa Cowan, *Walking the Same Hallways: Youth Leadership for College Access* (New York: College Access: Research & CARA, Brooklyn Community Foundation, 2012), 13–14.
25. Andrew S. Latham, "Peer Counseling: Proceed with Caution," *Educational Leadership* 55, no. 2 (1997): 77.
26. American School Counselor Association, *The School Counselor and Peer Support Programs* (Alexandria, VA: ASCA, 2015), 1.
27. Sharon Robinson et al., "Peer Counselors in a High School Setting: Evaluation of Training and Impact on Students," *The School Counselor* 39, no. 1 (1991): 35.
28. For additional examples, see https://www.edutopia.org/practice/student-led-conferences-empowerment-and-ownership.
29. Laura Smith, Kathryn Davis, and Malika Bhowmik, "Youth Participatory Action

Research Groups as School Counseling Interventions," *Professional School Counseling* 14, no. 2 (2010): 175.

30. Julio Cammarota and Michelle Fine, "Youth Participatory Action Research: A Pedagogy for Transformational Resistance," in *Revolutionizing Education: Youth Participatory Action Research in Motion*, eds. Julio Cammarota and Michelle Fine (New York: Routledge, 2008), 2.

31. Cammarota and Fine, *Revolutionizing Education*, 2.

32. Smith, Davis, and Bhowmik, "Youth Participatory Action Research Groups," 176; A small number of articles have addressed YPAR in relation to the work of school psychologists and other school-based counseling professionals.

33. Smith, Davis, and Bhowmik, "Youth Participatory Action Research Groups," 177.

34. Dana C. Gillilan, "Parental Perceptions of Elementary School Counselors in a Suburban Atlanta School, " *Georgia School Counselors Association Journal* 13, no. 1 (2006): 44.

35. David W. Chapman, Mary DeMasi, and Cynthia O'Brien, "Parents' Perceptions of the Effectiveness of Public School Counselors in College Advising," *The School Counselor* 38, no. 4 (1991): 275.

36. Aviva Shimoni and Lori Greenberger, *The Professional Message Delivered by School Counselors: Delivering the Information About School Counselors and School Counseling* (Kfar Saba, Israel: Beit Berl College, Research and Evaluation Unit, 2010).

37. Marissa Martinelli, "Controversial Depiction of Teen Suicide Has School Counselors Picking Up Pieces," *Slate*, May 1, 2017, http://www.slate.com/blogs/browbeat/2017/05/01/school_counselors_talk_netflix_s_controversial_teen_suicide_drama_13_reasons.html.

38. US Department of Education, *Issue Brief: Student Support Teams* (Washington, DC: US Department of Education, Office of Planning, Evaluation and Policy Development, 2017), 1.

39. US Department of Defense Education Activity, *Guidelines for Student Support Teams* (Arlington, VA: US Department of Defense Education Activity, 2007), 5.

40. US Department of Defense Education Activity, *Guidelines*, 5.

41. US Department of Education, *Issue Brief*, 4–5.

42. US Department of Education, 3.

43. US Department of Education, 4.

44. Manuel French and Eric Williams, "Postsecondary Leadership Team (PLT): Driving Student Support and Outcomes" (presentation at the 2015 College Changes Everything Conference, Tinley Park, IL, 2015).

45. Eric Williams, "Postsecondary Leadership Teams: Collaborating in the Southwest Network for College Awareness, Readiness, Access, and Success" (presentation at the Summer Counselor Institute, Chicago, IL, 2012).

46. New York City Department of Education, *College Access for All: Building a College-*

and Career-Ready Culture in Every New York City Public School (New York: NYCDOE, Office of Postsecondary Readiness, 2018), 1–2.

Chapter 4

1. Doreen Finkelstein, *A Closer Look at the Principal–Counselor Relationship: A Survey of Principals and Counselors* (Washington, DC: The College Board, 2009), 4.
2. Finkelstein, *A Closer Look*, 4.
3. Finkelstein, 4–7.
4. American School Counselor Association, "Annual Agreement Template," https://www. schoolcounselor.org/asca/media/asca/ASCA%20National%20Model%20Templates/ AnnualAgreementTemplate.pdf.
5. For more information, see https://www.schoolcounselor.org/school-counselors-members/asca-national-model.
6. American School Counselor Association, *ASCA National Model: A Framework for School Counseling Programs*, 3rd ed. (Alexandria, VA: ASCA, 2012), 24.
7. Melissa Clinedinst and Anna-Maria Koranteng, *2017 State of College Admission* (Arlington, VA: National Association for College Admission Counseling, 2017), 37.
8. The College Board National Office for School and Counselor Advocacy, *The College Board 2012 National Survey of School Counselors and Administrators: Report on Survey Findings: Barriers and Supports to School Counselor Success* (Washington, DC: NOSCA, 2012), 18.
9. Scott E. Carrell and Susan A. Carrell, "Do Lower Student to Counselor Ratios Reduce School Disciplinary Problems?" *Contributions to Economic Analysis & Policy* 5, no. 1 (2006): 7–11; Richard T. Lapan, Norman C. Gysbers, Stanley Bragg, and Margaret E. Pierce, "Missouri Professional School Counselors: Ratios Matter, Especially in High-Poverty Schools," *Professional School Counseling* 16, no. 2 (2012): 111–13; Chung Pham and Tracy Keenan, "Counseling and College Matriculation: Does the Availability of Counseling Affect College-Going Decisions Among Highly Qualified First-Generation College-Bound High School Graduates?" *Journal of Applied Economics and Business Research* 1, no. 1 (2011): 16–18.
10. John Carey et al., "A Statewide Evaluation of the Outcomes of the Implementation of ASCA National Model School Counseling Programs in Utah High Schools," *Professional School Counseling* 16, no. 2 (2012): 95–96.
11. Michael Hurwitz and Jessica Howell, "Estimating Causal Impacts of School Counselors with Regression Discontinuity Designs," *Journal of Counseling & Development* 92, no. 3 (2014): 320–23.
12. National Association for College Admission Counseling & American School Counselor Association, *State-by-State Student-to-Counselor Ratio Report: 10-Year Trends* (Arlington, VA, 2018: NACAC), 1.
13. American School Counselor Association, *The School Counselor and Comprehensive School Counseling Programs* (Alexandria, VA: 2017), 1.

14. Douglas J. Gagnon and Marybeth J. Mattingly, *Most U.S. Districts Have Low Access to School Counselors*, National Issue Brief #108 (Durham, NH: University of New Hampshire, Carsey School of Public Policy, 2016), 3.

15. Gagnon and Mattingly, *Most U.S. Districts*, 2.

16. Colorado Department of Education, "School Counselor Corps Grant Program," https://www.cde.state.co.us/postsecondary/schoolcounselorcorps.

17. Sheila Arredondo, Dan Jesse, Shelley H. Billig, and Jennifer Weston-Sementelli, *Colorado School Counselor Corps Grant Program: Early Experiences and Lessons Learned* (San Francisco, CA: WestEd, 2016), 1.

18. Colorado Department of Education, *2017 Legislative Report Colorado School Counseling Corps Grant Program* (Denver, CO: CDE), 5.

19. Alexandria Walton Radford, Nicole Ilfill, and Terry Lew, *A National Look at the High School Counseling Office: What Is It Doing and What Role Can It Play in Facilitating Students' Paths to College?* (Washington, DC: National Association for College Admission Counseling, 2012), 4.

20. Norman C. Gysbers and Patricia Henderson, *Developing and Managing Your School Guidance and Counseling Program* (Alexandria, VA: American Counseling Association, 2012), 231.

21. Gysbers and Henderson, *Developing and Managing*, 230.

22. Gysbers and Henderson, 23.

23. Arne Duncan, Dear colleague letter, June 30, 2014, https://www2.ed.gov/policy/elsec/guid/secletter/140630.html.

Chapter 5

1. American School Counselor Association, *ASCA National Model: A Framework for School Counseling Programs Executive Summary*, 3rd ed. (Alexandria, VA: ASCA, 2012), 1.

2. For an extensive review of data-driven school counseling practices, see Trish Hatch, *The Use of Data in School Counseling: Hatching Results for Students, Programs, and the Profession* (Thousand Oaks, CA: Corwin, 2014).

3. The College Board National Office for School Counselor Advocacy, *2012 National Survey of School Counselors: True North: Charting the Course to College and Career Readiness* (Washington, DC: College Board, 2012), 16.

4. Melissa A. Maras et al., "Measuring Evaluation Competency Among School Counselors," *Counseling Outcome Research and Evaluation* 4, no. 2 (2013): 104; Anita Young and Carol Kaffenberger, "School Counseling Professional Development: Assessing the Use of Data to Inform School Counseling Services," *Professional School Counseling* 19, no. 1 (2015): 52; Randall L. Astramovich, "Program Evaluation Interest and Skills of School Counselors," *Professional School Counseling* 20, no. 1 (2016): 59.

5. Cheryl Holcomb-McCoy, *School Counseling to Close the Achievement Gap: A Social Justice Framework for Success* (Thousand Oaks, CA: Corwin Press, 2007), 81–94.

6. Chrys Dougherty, *How School District Leaders Can Support the Use of Data to Improve Teaching and Learning Issue Brief* (Iowa City, IA: ACT, 2015), 2–4.

7. Dougherty, *How School District Leaders Can Support*, 2–4.

8. Carol Kaffenberger, "Designated Data Mondays," *ASCA School Counselor* (January/February 2014): 19.

9. Melissa Clinedinst and Anna Koranteng, *2017 State of College Admission* (Arlington, VA: National Association for College Admission Counseling, 2017), 24.

10. Richard DuFour, Robert Eaker, Rebecca DuFour, and Gayle Karhanek, *Whatever It Takes: How Professional Learning Communities Respond When Kids Don't Learn* (Bloomington, IN: National Education Service, 2004), 4.

11. Jennifer Barrow and Nancy Mamlin, "Collaboration Between Professional School Counselors and Special Education Teachers," *VISTAS*, no. 42 (2016): 5.

12. "Guidance Counselor," The Princeton Review, https://www.princetonreview.com/careers/75/guidance-counselor.

13. Glenn W. Lambie, "The Contribution of Ego Development Level to Burnout in School Counselors: Implications for Professional School Counseling," *Journal of Counseling and Development* 85, no. 1 (2007): 82; Doris S. DeMato and Claire Cole Curcio, "Job Satisfaction of Elementary School Counselors: A New Look," *Professional School Counseling* 7, no. 4 (2004): 240–41; Christopher McCarthy et al., "An Exploration of School Counselors' Demands and Resources: Relationship to Stress, Biographic, and Caseload Characteristics," *Professional School Counseling* 13, no. 3 (2010): 154–55.

14. Patrick R. Mullen and Daniel Gutierrez, "Burnout, Stress and Direct Student Services Among School Counselors," *The Professional Counselor* 6, no. 4 (2016): 352.

Chapter 6

1. EdVestors and BPS Visual & Performing Arts Department, *Dancing to the Top: How Collective Action Revitalized Arts Education in Boston* (Boston, MA: EdVestors), 2.

2. EdVestors and BPS Visual & Performing Arts Department, *Dancing to the Top*, 2.

3. Carol Johnson, "Schools at the Hub" (speech, Full-Service Roundtable, Boston, MA, February 2, 2012).

4. Kevin K. Kumashiro, "When Billionaires Become Educational Experts," *Academe*, May–June 2012, https://www.aaup.org/article/when-billionaires-become-educational-experts#.W225o9hKgnV.

5. Sarah Reckhow, *Follow the Money: How Foundation Dollars Change Public School Politics* (Oxford, UK: Oxford University Press, 2013), 6–7.

6. Inside Philanthropy, "College Readiness Funders," https://www.insidephilanthropy.com/grants-for-college-readin/.

7. Institute for Higher Education Policy, *Corporate Investment in College Readiness and Access* (Washington, DC: IHEP, 2008), 10.

8. Nicole Cammack et al., "Funding Expanded School Mental Health Programs," in

Handbook of School Mental Health: Research, Training, Practice, and Policy, 2nd ed., eds. Mark D. Weist et al. (Boston, MA: Springer, 2014), 20.

9. Cammack et al., "Funding Expanded," 20.

10. Reckhow, *Follow the Money,* 7.

11. Stats Indiana, "Indiana In-depth Profile," http://www.stats.indiana.edu/profiles/profiles.asp?scope_choice=a&county_changer=18000.

12. The Annie E. Casey Foundation, *Kids Count Data Book 2016* (Baltimore, MD: The Annie E. Casey Foundation, 2016), 19.

13. Indiana Chamber of Commerce Foundation, *Indiana School Counseling Research Review* (Indianapolis, IN: ICC, 2014), 30–31.

14. Lilly Endowment Inc., *Comprehensive Counseling Initiative for Indiana K–12 Students Request for Proposals Counseling Initiative Round II* (Indianapolis, IN: Lilly Endowment, Inc., 2017), 3.

15. Lilly Endowment Inc., "Lilly Endowment Announces $26.4 Million in Counseling Grants to School Corporations and Charter Schools Statewide," news release, September 29, 2017, http://www.lillyendowment.org/pdf/COUNSELING2017.pdf.

16. At the time of this publication, the initiative had not yet been evaluated.

17. Nancy Bodenhorn, "Facilitating Personal and Social Development," in *Handbook of School Counseling,* eds. Hardin L. K. Coleman and Christine Yeh (Abingdon, UK: Routledge, 2008), 214.

18. The College Board National Office for School Counselor Advocacy, *School Counselors: Literature and Landscape Review* (Washington, DC: NOSCA, 2011), 27.

19. Renée L. Rider to BOCES District Superintendents, Superintendents of Public School Districts, Principals of Public Schools, School Counselors, January 3, 2018, *Amendments to the Commissioner's Regulations Related to School Counseling,* http://www.p12.nysed.gov/sss/SchoolCounselingMemo.html.

20. Colorado Department of Education, *2017 Legislative Report Colorado School Counseling Corps Grant Program* (Denver, CA: CDE), 5.

21. Colorado Department of Education, "School Counselor Corps Grant Program," https://www.cde.state.co.us/postsecondary/schoolcounselorcorps.

22. Colorado Department of Education, *2016 Legislative Report Colorado School Counseling Corps Grant Program* (Denver, CA: CDE, 2016), 14.

23. These following states mandate school counseling for K–8: AL, AR, DE, DC, GA, ID, IN, IA, ME, MD, MO, MS, MT, NE, NH, NJ, NM, NY, OK, OR, RI, TN, VT, VA, WV, WI, WY.

24. These following states mandate school counseling for K–12: AL, AR, DE, DC, GA, ID, IN, IA, LA, ME, MD, MO, MS, MT, NE, NV, NH, NJ, NM, NY, ND, OK, OR, RI, SC, TN, UT, VT, VA, WA, WV, WI, WY.

25. American School Counselor Association, "State School Counseling Mandates and Legislation," https://www.schoolcounselor.org/school-counselors-members/careers-roles/state-school-counseling-mandates-and-legislation.

26. American School Counselor Association, "State School Counseling."

27. Ian Martin, John Carey, and Karen DeCoster, "A National Study of the Current Status of State School Counseling Models," *Professional School Counseling* 12, no. 5 (2009): 381.

28. The Carl D. Perkins Career and Technical Education Act of 2006 provides federal funding to school districts' career and technical education programs.

29. Utah State Board of Education, *College and Career Readiness Counseling Model*, 2nd ed. (Salt Lake City, UT: Utah State Board of Education, 2016), 2.

30. Utah State Board of Education, *College and Career Readiness Counseling Model*, 63.

31. Utah State Board of Education, 2.

32. US Department of Education, "Table 219. Public High School 4-Year Adjusted Cohort Graduation Rate (ACGR), by Selected Student Characteristics and State: 2010–11 through 2015–16," https://nces.ed.gov/ccd/tables/ACGR_RE_and_characteristics_2013-14.asp; American School Counselor Association, *Student-to-School Counselor Ratio 2015–2016* (Alexandria, VA: ASCA, 2018), 1.

33. Richard T. Lapan et al., "Missouri Professional School Counselors; Ratios Matter, Especially in High-Poverty Schools," *Professional School Counseling* 16, no. 2 (2012): 112–13.

34. Institute of Education Sciences and National Center for Education Statistics, "Table 1. Public High School 4-Year Adjusted Cohort Graduation Rate (ACGR), by Race/Ethnicity and Selected Demographics for the United States, the 50 States, and the District of Columbia: School Year 2013–14," Common Core of Data, https://nces.ed.gov/ccd/tables/ACGR_RE_and_characteristics_2013-14.asp.

35. Institute of Education Sciences and National Center for Education Statistics, "Table 1."

36. Bragg Stanley, *MSIP 5: Implications for Guidance and Counseling* (Jefferson City, MO: Missouri Department of Elementary and Secondary Education, 2013), 2.

37. Minnesota Senate, 89th Legislature, S.F. 1364, *Student Support Services Personnel Act*, 2015, https://www.revisor.mn.gov/bills/text.php?number=SF1364&version=0&session_year=2015&session_number=0.

38. Norman C. Gysbers et al., *Missouri Comprehensive School Counseling Program* (Jefferson City, MO: Missouri Department of Elementary and Secondary Education, 2017), 2.

39. Gysbers et al., *Missouri Comprehensive School Counseling Program*, 12.

40. US Department of Labor, "Individualized Learning Plans Across the U.S.," https://www.dol.gov/odep/ilp/map/.

41. Hobsons & National Association for College Admission Counseling, *Individualized Learning Plans for College and Career Readiness: State Policies and School-Based Practices, A National Study* (Arlington, VA: Hobsons, 2015), 2.

42. V. Scott Solberg et al., *Use of Individualized Learning Plans as a Promising Practice for Driving College and Career Readiness Efforts: Findings and Recommendations from a*

Multi-Method, Multi-Study Effort (Washington, DC: National Collaborative on Workforce and Disability for Youth, Institute for Educational Leadership, 2014), 4.

43. US Department of Labor, "Individualized Learning Plans Across the U.S."

44. National Collaborative on Workforce and Disability, "Individualized Learning Plans," http://www.ncwd-youth.info/fact-sheet/individualized-learning-plan.

45. Hobsons & National Association for College Admission Counseling, *Individualized Learning Plans for College and Career Readiness*, 11.

46. Hobsons & National Association for College Admission Counseling, 11.

47. US Department of Education, *Non-Regulatory Guidance Student Support and Academic Enrichment Grants* (Washington, DC: Department of Education, 2016), 4–5.

48. William J. Taggart, US Department of Education, Federal Student Aid, to Secondary School Administrators, April 13, 2010, https://www2.ed.gov/finaid/info/apply/fafsa-project.html.

49. Laura Owen and Erik Westlund, "Increasing College Opportunity: School Counselors and FAFSA Completion," *Journal of College Access* 2, no. 1 (2016): 11.

50. US Department of Education, *Education Department Launches New Data Tool to Help High School Officials Increase FAFSA Completion and College Accessibility* (Washington, DC: US Department of Education, 2012).

51. Federal Student Aid, US Department of Education, "Find FAFSA Completion Data About Your High School," https://financialaidtoolkit.ed.gov/tk/learn/fafsa/completion.jsp.

52. EdVestors and BPS Visual & Performing Arts Department, *Dancing to the Top*, 2.

Conclusion

1. Chung Pham and Tracy Keenan, "Counseling and College Matriculation: Does the Availability of Counseling Affect College-Going Decisions Among Highly Qualified First-Generation College-Bound High School Graduates?" *Journal of Applied Economics and Business Research* 1, no. 1 (2011): 18–19.

2. US Department of Education, Office for Civil Rights, *A First Look: Key Data Highlights on Equity and Opportunity Gaps in Our Nation's Public Schools* (Washington, DC: US Department of Education, 2016), 1.

3. Alexandria Walton Radford, Nicole Ilfill, and Terry Lew, *A National Look at the High School Counseling Office: What Is It Doing and What Role Can It Play in Facilitating Students' Paths to College?* (Arlington, VA: National Association for College Admission Counseling, 2014), 6.

4. Cathy A. Toll, *Literacy Coach's Survival Guide: Essential Questions and Practical Answers*, 2nd ed. (Newark, DE: International Reading Association, 2014), 10.

5. National Center for Homeless Education, *Sex Trafficking of Minors: What Schools Need to Know to Recognize and Respond to the Trafficking of Students* (Washington, DC: NCHE), 5.

6. DataUSA, "Counselors," https://datausa.io/profile/soc/211010/#education.

7. College Board National Office for School Counselor Advocacy, *2012 National Survey of School Counselors: True North: Charting the Course to College and Career Readiness* (Washington, DC: College Board, 2012), 78–79.

8. College Board National Office for School Counselor Advocacy, *National Survey of School Counselors*, 79.

9. Aviva Shimoni and Lori Greenberger, "School Counselors Deliver Information About School Counseling and Their Work," *Professional School Counseling* 18, no. 1 (2014): 23–24.

10. Shimoni and Greenberger, "School Counselors Deliver Information," 25.

11. Shimoni and Greenberger, 25.

ACKNOWLEDGMENTS

At the outset, I would like to thank the many educators who contributed to this book by sharing their stories and efforts to improve students' educational experiences. In particular, special thanks go to Rouel Belleza, Erin Bibo-Ward, Janice Bloom, Lori Chajet, Nicole Cobb, Danielle Duarte, Kimberly Hanauer, Samantha Haviland, Jillian Kelton, Dave Lewis, Toby Marston, Laura Perille, Judy Petersen, Marinell Rousmaniere, Traci Small, and Eric Waldo. Learning about the great work happening around the country was the highlight of this project.

The idea to write this book came from my editor at the Harvard Education Press, Caroline Chauncey. Caroline had the great wisdom and heart to discourage me from following my initial writing plan and instead to write about school counseling, something she could see I was passionate about. This was the second time I had to be nudged to write about this topic. The first came from my doctoral dissertation director and friend, Ana Martínez-Alemán. Both of these women observed that I was itching to tell a story about school counselors that I believed the field was lacking and offered just the right amount of encouragement for me to do it. I am incredibly grateful to both of them.

Like students' experiences in school, I benefitted from a network of people who offered support and encouragement at various points in the development of this book. My "professional home" consists of friends and colleagues, including Roberta Bassett, Karen Bottari, Gretchen Brion-Meisels, Heather Rowan-Kenyon, Marinell Rousmaniere, and Francesca Purcell. I'd also like to thank Tara Nicola for her optimistic attitude and tenacious work ethic. Tara arrived at HGSE just in time to play a big part in this project. Pei Pei Liu, Dean Redfearn, Anne Blevins, and the staff at the Harvard Education Press offered valuable support along the way.

I am eternally grateful to Suzanne Bouffard, whose enthusiasm, guidance, and developmental editing have been essential to the completion of this book.

Others who helped guide the project in meaningful ways include my partners in this work: Laura Owen, Trish Hatch, Cheryl Holcomb-McCoy, Alice Anne

Bailey, Pat Martin, Joyce Brown, Greg Darneider, and Bridget Terry Long. I thank them all for their important leadership in the field of school counseling and postsecondary readiness.

I am especially thankful to my family, whose love and support give me the courage to take on big projects like writing a book on top of the millions of other demands in our lives. I appreciate Sydney for her artwork and nudges to send particular emails, Lilly for giving me writing goals each day, and Ruby for leaving me surprise doodles on my work.

Finally, I would like to thank my husband, Toby, without whom this book would not have happened. He is critical at all the right times and unwavering in his support for me at all the others. Toby understands the complexities of education better than anyone I know. He informed this book, both in substance and form, more than anyone. He is, and will always be, my home.

ABOUT THE AUTHOR

Mandy Savitz-Romer is the Nancy Pforzheimer Aronson Senior Lecturer in Human Development and Education at the Harvard Graduate School of Education. As a former urban high school counselor, Savitz-Romer is particularly interested in how schools and districts structure counseling support systems and college planning efforts to reach all students. Her writing and research link research to practice in the field of school counseling, specifically as it relates to postsecondary transitions and success for first-generation college students. Savitz-Romer has also held teaching and administrative positions at Boston College, Boston University, Simmons College, and the Boston Higher Education Partnership. She is the coauthor of *Ready, Willing, and Able: A Developmental Approach to College Success* and *Technology and Engagement: Making Technology Work for First Generation College Students*. Savitz-Romer holds a PhD in higher education from Boston College and a master's degree in school counseling from Boston University.

INDEX

Boston Public Schools Arts Expansion,
152, 154, 156–157, 160, 176–177
buddy programs, 83
bullying, 9, 31, 172, 190
burnout, 144–145
Bush, George W., 38

CARA. *See* College Access: Research and
Action
care coordination, 55–58, 86–87
career and technical education (CTE), 28,
45, 166, 184–185
career development, 25–28
career readiness, 2, 13–14, 33–36
Carey, John, 39, 192
Carl D. Perkins Vocational Education
Act, 45
cascade theory, 59
caseloads, 11, 17, 62, 116–118, 168–169,
181
Center for School Counseling Outcome
Research and Evaluation (CSCORE),
39, 192
charter schools, 154–155
Cherokee County School District, 142–
143, 185
CLGs. *See* counselor learning groups
coalition building, 68, 187–190
Cobb, Nicole, 129–131, 188
collaboration, 57–58, 131, 187, 188–189
collective bargaining, 116
collective impact models, 96
college access programs, 12–13, 77
College Access: Research and Action
(CARA), 81–82
College Board, 33, 34, 43, 74, 103, 114
college counseling, 33–36, 182
"college for all" philosophy, 28, 33
college planning, 4, 17, 28, 76, 77, 87, 181
college readiness, 2, 13–14, 33–36, 154
Colorado, 164–165

communication, 87–91, 104, 189–190
community-based programs, 155–156
community building, 183–187
community partners, 63, 64, 69, 76–80,
94–95, 188–189
community schools, 59
community youth programs, 12–13
comprehensive care, 58–59, 64
Comprehensive Counseling Initiative,
158–159, 160
content specialization assignment,
119–120
Council for Accreditation of Counseling
and Related Educational Programs,
43
Council of National School Counseling
and College Access Organizations,
44
Counseling at the Crossroads report, 43
counseling community, 183–187
counseling models, 41–42
counseling psychology, 28–29
The Counselor in a Changing World
(Wrenn), 29
counselor learning groups (CLGs),
142–143
crises management, 30, 144
CSCORE. *See* Center for School
Counseling Outcome Research and
Evaluation
CTE. *See* career and technical education

Dahir, Carol, 46
data-driven systems, 61, 133–138,
174–176
Denver Public Schools, 125–126, 139
departmental alignment, 130–131
depression, 2, 30, 31, 80
DeWitt Wallace-Reader's Digest Fund, 43
Dimmitt, Carey, 39, 192
distributive counseling, 71–74

school leaders, *continued*
  enactment of academic home model by,
    109–122
  expectations for counselors of, 102–107
  performance evaluations and, 146–148
  positioning of school counseling
    programs by, 107–109
  professional development and, 120–122
  role of, 101–102
  student-counselor assignments and,
    118–120
schools
  charter, 154–155
  community, 59
  core mission of, 1–2
  expectations for, 1, 2, 18, 46, 180
  financial support of, 153–154
  high-poverty, 181–182
  mission statements of, 110–113
  private philanthropy and, 153–162
  rural, 61–62, 191
  as systems, 6
school safety, 30, 32
Schools and Staffing Survey (SASS), 117
school shootings/violence, 15, 31, 32
school transitions, 93, 162
school websites, 87–88
Schwartz, Bob, 28
self-care, 144–145
"senior walk," 83
Sexton, Thomas, 38
social capital, 54–55
social emotional learning (SEL), 14,
  161–162
social emotional support, 28–30, 32
social justice, 37
social needs, 1, 2
social service agencies, 12–13, 15, 32, 56,
  77–78
social workers, 32

Society for the Prevention of Teen Suicide,
  89
specialists, 55, 56, 62–63, 70
specialized counselors, 36
specialized services, 76–80
Sputnik, 19, 44, 45, 46, 173
SSAE. *See* Student Support and Academic
  Enrichment (SSAE) grants
standards-based movement, 36–37
standards-driven decision making, 61
state boards of education, 169–172
state policies, 20, 163–173
static assignment, 119
student achievement, 15–16, 36–40, 179
student-centered learning, 53
student-counselor assignments, 118–120
student development, 59, 60
student-led conferences, 83–85
students
  communication with, 88–90
  diverse needs of, 2–3
  diverse populations of, 72
  first-generation college, 181
  high-risk, 15–16, 70
  low-income, 16, 17, 33, 34–35, 180–181
  mental health issues in, 30–32
  minority, 17, 30, 181
  partnering with, 69, 80–86
  social emotional support for, 28–30
  time with, as priority, 113–116
  transgender/gender non-conforming,
    30
  transitions for, 93, 162
  undocumented, 50, 56–57
Student Support and Academic
  Enrichment (SSAE) grants, 9, 174
student support services, coordination of,
  55–58
Student Support Services Personnel Act,
  169